国际和平城市
丛书

International Cities of Peace

国家出版基金项目
江苏省"十四五"重点图书出版规划项目
侵华日军南京大屠杀遇难同胞纪念馆资助项目

COVENTRY

英国
考文垂

UK

International Cities of Peace

Series Editor: Liu Cheng
Associate Editors: Ling Xi   Chen Junfeng

Elly Harrowell

南京师范大学出版社

United Nations Educational, Scientific and Cultural Organization
UNESCO Chair on Peace Studies
Nanjing University
People's Republic of China

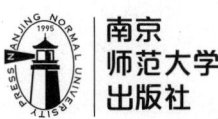

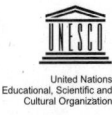

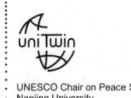

图书在版编目（CIP）数据

英国·考文垂= Coventry, UK：英文／（英）艾莉·哈罗维尔（Elly Harrowell）著. -- 南京：南京师范大学出版社, 2022.8
（国际和平城市丛书／刘成主编）
ISBN 978-7-5651-5405-8

Ⅰ. ①英… Ⅱ. ①艾… Ⅲ. ①城市—概况—英国—英文 Ⅳ. ①K956.1

中国版本图书馆CIP数据核字（2022）第135143号

丛 书 名	国际和平城市丛书
丛书主编	刘　成
丛书副主编	凌　曦　陈俊峰
书　　名	Coventry, UK
著　　者	［英］艾莉·哈罗维尔（Elly Harrowell）
策划编辑	徐　蕾　郑海燕
责任编辑	彭　茜
书籍设计	瀚清堂
出版发行	南京师范大学出版社
地　　址	江苏省南京市玄武区后宰门西村9号（邮编：210016）
电　　话	（025）83598712（编辑部）83598919（总编办）83598412（营销部）
网　　址	http://press.njnu.edu.cn
电子信箱	nspzbb@njnu.edu.cn
照　　排	南京私书坊文化传播有限公司
印　　刷	上海雅昌艺术印刷有限公司
开　　本	889毫米×1194毫米　1/32
印　　张	4.75
版　　次	2022年8月第1版　2022年8月第1次印刷
书　　号	ISBN 978-7-5651-5405-8
定　　价	50.00元
出 版 人	张志刚

* 南京师大版图书若有印装问题请与销售商调换
* 版权所有　侵犯必究

Foreword by Series Editor

This book series, International Cities of Peace, Volume I, introduces five cities, which have one thing in common that they have all experienced the trauma of war in their history, and the collective memories have endured from one generation to the next. So, history must be kept in mind. Only by looking back on past sufferings and using history as a mirror can we prevent such historical tragedies from occurring again. It is absolutely vital to recognize and remember the historical trauma, but how we remember it may affect its authenticity and how long we will keep it in mind. According to history, building peace is the best remedy for remembering and recovering from the past suffering. When the traumatic memory of a city is transformed into a common human memory, we can understand the past disasters in a new way beyond stereotyped political memory. Only this can enable the traumatic history to be linked to the future peace, which can promote the reconciliation between the former hostile parties, and boost hope to the establishment of a community with a shared future for mankind. History indicates that reconciliation means not only exchanging our views and experiences of the past, but also a process of mutually creating new ideas for the future and sharing new experiences. In this way, reconciliation is a thought and a power that meets our mutual needs, which can be developed by building cities of peace with the legacy bequeathed by the war. That is why we wrote these books.

All the five cities of the book series are actively engaged in building a culture of peace. Nanjing, the first International City of Peace in China, held an international peace forum on positive peace; Dresden reflects on the war experience of Germany and strengthens domestic and international reconciliation; Hiroshima leads non-governmentally the anti-nuclear peace movement in Japan; Warsaw promotes the reconciliation dialogue that has led to a shared historical memory both inside and outside Poland; Coventry is the benchmark for British reconciliation. At the same time, the study of war memory is undergoing changes in three dimensions: shifts from the hero memory to the traumatic memory, from the memory of a victorious country to the memory of all the wounded countries, and from the domestic historical memory of a country to historical memory shared by many countries. Our belief is that the memory of war will be ultimately eclipsed by the memory of peace, as more and more cities work towards building cities of peace and thus form a global network of peace cities.

The five cities have their own characteristics in building a city of peace. Their practice of building peace has proven the truth that "There is no way to peace; peace is the way". Cities of peace all share a common purpose, promoting the culture of peace advocated by UNESCO, that is, working to build peace through conflict prevention, mediation and transformation; providing peace education on non-violence, tolerance, acceptance, respect and sustainable development; promoting intercultural dialogue and reconciliation. To build a city of peace requires the joint efforts of governments, universities, social groups, non-government organizations and citizens from all countries and regions around the world, for it needs to incorporate elements of peace in historical records, memories and heritage. It can be achieved in many ways, such as conflict prevention, peace-keeping, peace-building, peace research, peace education, and all peace activities that promote urban progress and prosperity as well as world peace and development.

This book series rests on its disciplinary foundation, Peace Studies. With the only UNESCO Chair on Peace Studies in China, Nanjing University is widely recognized as the center of China's Peace Studies. The development of China's Peace Studies has received great help from many institutions and individuals around the world. Without their support, Peace Studies would not have developed in China, and these books would not have been published, either. This book series took ten years to compile, experiencing ups and downs along the way, and finally came out. All the authors, translators and editors have done their best to bring out these books against all the odds, and make them authentic, scholarly, innovative, and readable at the same time.

This book series is an attempt to understand how cultural trauma and historical memory affect us. We sincerely welcome readers to point out and correct the defects and mistakes in these books.

Liu Cheng
Professor, School of History, Nanjing University
Chairholder of UNESCO Chair on Peace Studies
August 2022

Contents

001

Foreword by Series Editor

008

Introduction

010

Chapter 1	Coventry before the War	
	A Brief History of Coventry	014
	Early Origins	015
	Industrial Coventry	023
	Coventry on the Eve of War	030

Chapter 2 The Coventry Blitz
The Calm before the Storm?	036
The 14th November: Devastation	039
A Cathedral "Ruined and Rebuilt"	043
Reconstruction and Rebirth	048

Chapter 3 Coventry's Peace Story: The Beginnings
Phoenix from the Flames: Coventry Cathedral's Rebirth as a Centre for Peace and Reconciliation	060
Rebuilding for Peace—The Reconstruction of Coventry Cathedral	067
Civic Leadership—Coventry City Council and the Pursuit of Peace	075
The Birth of City Twinning	076
Coventry's Civil Defence Controversy	082
A Conference for Peace	084
1962 onwards—The Growing Role of Civil Society	087

Chapter 4 From the International to the Local: Civil Society Takes up the Challenge of Peace

People-to-people Peace—The Coventry Committee for
    International Understanding   094
Industrial Decline and the End of the Golden Age for Peace?   098
Confronting Racism—The Fight for Peace Begins at Home   102
The Rise of Civil Society Peace Activists   104
Coventry Peace House   105
The Lord Mayor's Committee for Peace and Reconciliation   107
The Positive Images Festival   109

Chapter 5 Turning to the Future and the Resurgence of the Peace Narrative

Coventry Cathedral's International Ministry—A Proactive
    Force on the International Stage   114
Establishing an Academic Centre for Peace in Coventry   118
Branding a City of Peace and Reconciliation—The Council
    Re-engages   122

128		
Chapter 6	**Looking to the future**	
	Threats to the Peace Narrative	134
	Lessons from Coventry	138

143

Main Bibliography

145

Acknowledgements

Introduction

How can a city and the people who live in it take the memory and experience of their darkest, most painful days and use them to fuel a commitment to pursuing peace with their former enemies? This is the question at the heart of this book. The city of Coventry, in the heart of England's Midlands region, took its place in the roll call of places devastated by the terrible violence of World War II after a single night of intense bombing, leaving the city center unrecognisable in 1940. However, it is the city's response to this tragedy, the path it has attempted to forge since then, that distinguishes Coventry. By calling for peace and forgiveness instead of revenge and further violence, and by putting in place a remarkable series of peace-focused initiatives in the years that followed, the city has carved a name for itself as a champion of peace and reconciliation.

This has not always been an easy task. As the city has changed, so has the world around it, and both have presented new challenges to the task of building a peaceful city. The focus of building peace in Coventry has shifted over time from reconciling with former foes in Germany, to resisting the divisions of the Cold War, to addressing tensions and injustice within the city itself. The work of achieving this peace has fallen to different people and institutions over the years, groups have often taken a markedly different approach to achieving this laudable aim. Of course, this has not been plain sailing—as we shall see, there have been challenges to this peace narrative along the way. This brief introduction to Coventry's story of peace and reconciliation aims to give an overview of the city's attempt to build a peaceful future from the ashes of war, and perhaps inspire others to do the same.

The book will begin by describing a little of Coventry's history and the forces that shaped the city as it stood at the brink of World War II. The second chapter will then detail the city's experience in November 1940; the destruction of the city centre that would in turn prompt Coventry's turn to peace. Chapter Three picks up the story in the aftermath of the bombing, and charts how a number of key institutions and committed individuals successfully used the city's wartime experiences to work for peace, often through innovative and courageous actions. In Chapter Four we discuss the further development of this peace narrative, particularly as Coventry's economic fortunes waned and new actors became increasingly involved in setting the city's peace agenda. Finally, Chapter Five examines the resurgence of the city's peace identity at the turn of the millennium, and offers some concluding thoughts about the challenges to, and achievements of, the city's commitment to peace and reconciliation.

Chapter 1
Coventry before the War

A Brief History of Coventry

The Coventry of today would be unrecognisable to someone who had seen the city received its Charter of Incorporation in 1345. At that time the newly minted city's population hovered around 7,000, and it was taking its first step to become one of medieval England's most important trading and manufacturing cities. Today, Coventry is home to 360,100 people—a population that is both younger and more diverse than the national average, although also less wealthy. It is "a city of welcome, a city of peace and reconciliation, a city of innovation and invention", quoting the winning bid the city submitted to become the UK's City of Culture for 2021. But how did Coventry come to be the city it is today?

This chapter presents a brief overview of the roots and history of the city—its development from the Middle Ages to the time when the disaster befell on it in 1940. This is important to understand, since Coventry's wartime experience was directly linked to its identity and history in two ways. Firstly, looking back helps us to understand its status as an important manufacturing city, closely tied to the automotive and engineering industries, and later to the arms industry. These factories were prime targets for bombing raids looking to cripple Britain's war economy (as we shall see in the next chapter). Secondly, we can trace the development of the city's beautifully preserved medieval city centre, the devastation of which by bombing caused such distress to city residents, and to the British people more generally.

Early Origins

Perhaps destruction and recovery have always been at the heart of Coventry's story—some of the earliest historical references to Coventry speak of a Saxon nunnery destroyed by the invading forces of the Danish King Canute. By 1043 though, it had been rebuilt as a Benedictine monastery (later to become St Mary's Cathedral) by the powerful Earl of Mercia, Leofric and his wife Lady Godiva, who were to become figures of great importance in Coventry's heritage and mythmaking. This was followed over the next century by the construction of Coventry Castle and two further monasteries in neighbouring Coombe and Stoneleigh, and of a lively community of merchants and tradesmen which developed around these institutions, particularly in

> **Sent to Coventry?**
>
> The phrase "to be sent to Coventry" is commonly used to describe someone you have attempted to cut off or ostracise—not the most flattering association for the city, you might think. In fact, this common saying has an interesting historical basis. During the English Civil War in the 17th century, Royalist prisoners were sent to Coventry to be held in isolation because of the city's imposing 2-mile long city walls. Whilst the city walls and the prisoners may now be no more than a detail of history, the memory of this time has been passed down to us through the idea of "sending someone to Coventry".

response to the Abbeys' production of wool. The city was also ideally placed in geographical terms—near a good source of water (the River Sherbourne), plentiful arable land, and close to important trading routes Watling Street and Fosse Way which had been established since the Roman era.

By 1345 Coventry was a thriving town of around 7,000 residents when it received its Charter of Incorporation—a document granting its independence and the right to govern itself—by King Edward III. In a demonstration of the city's newfound rights, Coventry's first mayor, John Ward, was elected in January 1346. However, further disaster was just around the corner as the city was struck, along with the rest of the country, with a terrible outbreak of the bubonic plague (colloquially known as the Black Death). Without reliable records it is difficult to assess the impact of this outbreak on the fledgling city, but some historians estimate fully one fifth of the population perished during the epidemic. However, despite this setback the city's development continued apace, rising to become England's fourth most important trading city by the beginning of the 15th century. Its rising profile was underlined by the fact that the city was twice designated as the country's capital, first by Henry IV in 1404 who summoned a parliament there to raise funds for his army, and again between 1456 and 1459 during the Wars of the Roses.

It is important to note that the city's relatively fast growth was likely to have attracted quite a high level of immigration, as a successful trading point and growing centre for merchants, craftsmen and artisans. For many Coventry residents today, this is an important element of the city's historical identity as a city of welcome and immigration. Having initially made its name as a centre of wool production and trade, Coventry would further expand into the textile industries over the coming centuries, bringing more wealth to the city. 1627 saw the establishment of a silk weavers' company in Coventry, and this—particularly as it developed into silk ribbon-making—grew to be the city's primary industry by the 18th century (as well as watchmaking, which began to flourish a little later). Again, it is likely that the arrival of Huguenot refugees fleeing persecution in France aided the growth of the silk industry.

Fig.1-1 The statue of Lady Godiva, situated in Coventry's city centre

It is striking that by the beginning of the 20th century, even after the city had reinvented itself as a leading force in the automotive industry, more than 3,000 people (mainly women) remained employed in the textile industry in Coventry. However, even as the city continued to grow, it was outpaced by its great regional rivals, notably Birmingham, as the Industrial Revolution took hold. Nonetheless, an observer at that time might have remarked on the architectural legacy of Coventry's rise to become an important merchant city in England.

Fig.1-2 The St Mary's Guildhall, situated in Coventry's city centre

Fig.1-3 Coventry's famous "three spires" as depicted in an engraving from 1840

HRIST CHURCH.

Principal among this legacy was St Mary's Guildhall [Fig.1-2], which still stands in the city centre today and represents perhaps the finest remaining example of a mediaeval guildhall in the UK. The Guildhall was where leading merchants and business people met to regulate trade, hold ceremonies and host visiting dignitaries. In a trading city such as Coventry, it was therefore a hugely important site. Coventry was also known as the city of three spires, referring to the distinctive spires of the churches of St. Michael (built in the 14th century and becoming St. Michael's Cathedral in 1918 before its emblematic destruction in the 1940 raids); Holy Trinity (first mentioned in written records in 1113 and rebuilt in the 14th century); and Christ which survived the 1940 Blitz, but was destroyed in a subsequent air raid on the 8th April 1941, leaving only the spire standing in the city centre today [Fig.1-4].

Fig.1-4 The remains of the "spires" today

Industrial Coventry

The Industrial Revolution swept Britain in the 18th and 19th centuries, leaving its mark on Coventry where new housing sprang up to accommodate the growing population, just as it did elsewhere. All the same, unlike many of its neighbours, the city retained much of its mediaeval heart and street pattern, as well as its traditional industries. But just as Coventry's stalwart ribbon-making and watchmaking seemed to finally be losing the battle against the fast pace of new industries, a new and innovative industry took root in the city, bringing a change that was to set a new course for Coventry right up until the World War II and beyond.

The bicycle industry arrived in Coventry in the 1860s, just in time to save the city's dwindling fortunes, and ushered in a new era in which the city would become one of the engineering and manufacturing powerhouses of the British economy. As Thoms and Donnelly put it in their overview of the city's industrial development, "between 1880 and 1914 Coventry rapidly emerged from an industrial craft-based economy to dependence upon the light engineering industries of the twentieth century". Crucially, because of the way that light industry grew out of Coventry's pre-existing manufacturing businesses, these factories (and the ones that would follow them later) developed within the city, not on the outskirts—a fact that would prove devastating for the city later on.

Fig.1-5 The early bicycles on display at the Coventry Transport Museum

Fig.1-6 Coventry Daimler Motorcycle Club

Fig.1-7 Aircraft workshop in World War II

From bicycle manufacturing followed cars, exemplified by the arrival of the Daimler factory in 1896 (taking over the premises of a former textile mill), to the point that by 1931 there were eleven separate car manufacturing firms operating in the city. The city also played an important role in the development of the fledgling aeronautics industry; the first "all British" plane being built in the city in 1909, and the father of the jet engine Frank Whittle is fondly remembered as a son of Coventry. Not surprisingly when the British government's thoughts turned to rearmament in the mid-1930s, Coventry was quickly identified as a key part in these plans, having already played a central role in supporting the war effort during World War I.

In 1936 the Government strongly encouraged representatives of the automotive industry from Coventry and other manufacturing cities in the Midlands to turn their focus to the production of aircraft engines. Accordingly, four new factories were opened in Coventry between 1936 and 1937, all with this aim in mind. As might be expected, Coventry's front line role in rearmament had a huge impact on the city and its workforce. During the six short years from 1932-1938 the number of people involved in the manufacture of vehicles and aircraft had exploded from 29,658 to 41,825, whilst other linked industries such as engineering and electrical communications saw similar massive increases. By the time war was declared in 1939, Coventry found itself at the heart of the country's military-industrial machine, a fact that may have been central to the city's economic success but also, as we shall see in Chapter Two, a key part of its downfall.

One other key aspect of Coventry's development between the two wars was the shift in local politics as the increasingly industrialised city followed the trend set at national level by shifting towards the left, a move which was underpinned by the rising influence of trades unions, and the rapidly expanding urban working class. By 1929, the city elected its first Labour MP, the Quaker and perhaps surprisingly pro-disarmament Philip Noel-Baker. A staunch opponent of war, Noel-Baker would go on to win the Nobel Peace Prize in 1959, having played a central role in setting up both the League of Nations and the United Nations. By 1937 the Labour Party had also taken control of the City Council, starting a period of Labour control of the city that would last until well after World War II.

Coventry on the Eve of War

What was Coventry like, then, on the eve of World War II? The city had grown considerably—at the time of the 1931 census its population stood at 175,511, of which almost 50,000 were employed in the booming manufacturing sector. Estimates suggest that by the outbreak of World War II this had leapt further to around 220,000, with new arrivals from Ireland and those parts of England and Scotland which were suffering from the effects of the great depression seeking employment in Coventry's resilient economy. Coventry's Irish population in particular increased significantly at this time, more than doubling in the decade between 1921 and 1931, and rose to almost 10,000 by 1951, which was another important part of the city's story of immigration. Even as large parts of the city retained their distinctive mediaeval architecture, this increasingly butted up against signs of the modern world, with streets being widened to make way for cars, and ever more factories making their mark on the city.

The historian Frederick Taylor captured the paradoxical nature of Coventry in the 1930s well, when he reported the famous British novelist J.B. Priestley's reflections on visiting Coventry in 1933. Having expressed his surprise at "how much of the past, in soaring stone and carved wood, still remains in the city", Priestley went on to capture the contradictions of the "picturesque remains of the old city which are besieged by an army of nuts, bolts, hammers, spanners, gauges, drills, and machine lathes, for in a thick ring around the ancient centre are the motorcar and cycle factories, the machine tool makers, the magneto

Fig.1-8 Examples of some of Coventry's heritage architecture to survive the war, next to the ruins of the Cathedral

manufacturers and the electro companies. Beyond them again are whole new quarters where the mechanics and fitters and turners and furnace men live in neat brick rows, and drink their beer in gigantic new public houses, and take their wives to gigantic new picture theatres". Even caught as it was between its dual identity as a cradle of rich historical heritage and manufacturing booming town at the cutting edge of new industries, few residents of Coventry would have foretold what would happen to the city next as Britain and much of the world entered a new period of terrible conflict.

2

Chapter 2
The Coventry Blitz

The Calm before the Storm?

Although the night of 14th November 1940 is emblematic when we talk about the bombing of Coventry—this being the fateful night when such terrible damage was inflicted on the city centre—the bombing of Coventry actually began much earlier.

After Britain declared war on 3rd September 1939, Coventry, like many other British cities, took steps to prepare for the conflict, and notably the threat of aerial bombardment. Air-raid wardens were appointed, gas masks distributed and shelters constructed, to the extent that McGrory notes that "by 14th November 1940 the National Emergency Committee had created enough trenches, basements and surface shelters in Coventry to accommodate 170,344 citizens". Large parts of the city were also camouflaged to make them more difficult to spot from the air, and black-out regulations were put into force across the city. Against this backdrop of preparation, and the fevered pitch of industrial production to support the war effort, the first bombs did not fall on Coventry until the summer of 1940. On June 25th the airfield at Ansty, about 5 miles northeast of Coventry was bombed, without loss of life. This was followed by the first bombing within the boundaries of Coventry properly on August 18th, when 14 high explosive bombs were dropped in the Cannon Hill and Canley areas of the city, destroying two buildings there. Over the coming months, this pattern of bombing would increase, becoming more deadly and more devastating as the months went on. By October the city was facing frequent raids, with 176 people killed in that month alone.

During this period, Coventry continued to play a vital role in the British war effort. As mentioned in Chapter One, the motor car manufacturers of the Midlands, including prominent Coventry firms, had been asked by the government to contribute to the rebuilding of the Royal Air Force (RAF) ahead of the coming war, by turning their expertise to aircraft manufacturing, particularly aircraft engines. This was carried out by the creation of so-called "Shadow Factories"—new factories paid for by the government but managed by the businesses, whose output would be strictly dedicated to the race for

---

A Forgotten Bombing

Often overshadowed by the trauma that followed in 1940, Coventry was in fact subject to another bombing on 25th August 1939. On this day a bomb planted by the IRA (Irish Republican Army) exploded in a central shopping street, Broadgate, killing 5 people and injuring 70 more. This attack was part of a campaign of sabotage (the S Plan) by the IRA to try and force the British to withdraw from Ireland, that some have suggested the tacit support of German intelligence. Two men, James McCormick and Peter Barnes were convicted and later executed for their role in the bombings, and newspapers at the time reported an upsurge in anti-Irish sentiment in the city, with its large and overwhelmingly peaceful Irish population bearing the brunt of residents' anger. However, the declaration of war a week later soon wiped this bombing from the front pages. It was only in 2015 that a memorial was erected for those who had died in the attack, following a campaign by their relatives.

rearmament. These factories continued to increase their output through these early bombing raids, and even through the more severe bombardments that were to follow. As Richardson notes, by 1943, they were producing 800 engines a month (four times more than originally envisaged) and employing huge numbers of workers. One notable effect of these factories was to drastically increase the number of women working in factories. One estimate suggests that the number of women working in the shadow factories more than tripled from 3,800 in 1939 to 13,900 in 1941. This revolution would have lasting consequences for women's roles in the workplace come the end of the war.

By November 1940, then, Coventry was no longer a stranger to World War II. City life had changed in significant ways because of the advent of war, from its economy and working life, to daily routines that now took into account bombing raids, black-out rules and other facts of life under the threat of bombardment. Many children from the city had experienced evacuation to the countryside as a safety measure, although many had also returned to the city after the early months of the war which had been proved quieter than expected. In fact, because of the city's booming factories and their role at the heart of the war economy, the city was actually prospering, with many skilled and semi-skilled factory workers earning significantly higher than the national average wage. Frederick Taylor quotes the Mass Observation unit's view of Coventry in early summer 1940, which described Coventry as a city of "smart clothes in the streets, prosperous-looking homes, busy public houses, crowded shops, long queues outside cinemas". Coventry was booming despite, indeed, largely because of the war. All the same, by autumn, the city was being targeted with increasingly frequent raids, which were taking their toll on the morale and wellbeing of the population. Few could have expected, however, the terrible events that were to befall the city on 14th November, and how this would change Coventry's path from then on.

The 14th November: Devastation

The sheer numbers of planes and munitions involved in the 14th November raid on Coventry—dubbed "Moonlight Sonata" by the Germans, after the famous Beethoven piece—dwarfed everything that had come before it. Lasting eleven hours, the attack comprised of around 450 aircraft which dropped roughly 500 tons of munitions on the city. This included 1,000 high explosive bombs and around 30,000 incendiaries, which would ultimately prove so devastating to the city's mediaeval architecture. The first warnings that planes had been sighted were received at around 7 pm. By 8 pm it had become clear that this raid was going to be quite different to those which had come previously. Waves of bombers were crossing the city from different directions, creating a near constant barrage of incendiaries, mines and heavy explosives, as the emergency services on the ground struggled to keep up. The raid was one of the first to use "pathfinder" planes—a small contingent of advance planes that dropped incendiary bombs on the city in order to light it up for the later, heavy bombers. Speaking to the BBC in 1977, one German officer described the sight that met him as he flew in to attack the city:

As we were flying over the Channel, we could clearly see Coventry burning, so the use of radio aids was practically unnecessary. We attacked at about half past two at night and there was no defence. There was very little flak and no night fighters and, when we reached the target, there was a huge sea of flames.

Another German airman later described the city thousands of metres below them as they made their approach as a "blood red speck" on the landscape that lit up the night sky. The response on the ground to this overwhelming display of firepower was soon shown to be inadequate. Even with the aid of neighbouring towns and cities, there were not enough fire crews to put out all the fires created by the incendiary bombs. Even when there were crews, there wasn't enough water to put out the fires—the steps taken to prepare water supplies for just such an emergency before the war had been quite inadequate, and the situation became even more grave when the canal in the city centre was damaged, removing a crucial source of water for fighting the rapidly spreading fires. What is more, the coordination of the response was severely hampered as communications were destroyed by the bombing, leading the emergency services to rely on messengers carrying information by hand, often at great personal danger. In short, Coventry's first responders were quickly overwhelmed and powerless to prevent major damage to the city.

Fig.2-1 Holy Trinity Church rises above a scene of devastation in Coventry following the Luftwaffe air raid on the night of 14/15th November 1940

By the time the "all clear" was sounded at 6:16 am, the city centre was in ruins. 554 people had been killed in one night, with over a thousand more injured and treated in the city's overflowing and often seriously damaged hospitals. 60,000 buildings had been destroyed or damaged, including more than half of the houses in the city. Many of Coventry's most iconic places now lay smouldering; in addition to the Cathedral, the Library, the historic shopping streets of Broadgate and Jordan Well, with their more recent glamorous additions such as the art deco Gaumont Cinema or the Owen a department store (symbols of Coventry's growing pre-war wealth) were all destroyed. Coventry's many factories were also badly affected, particularly those located in the historic centre (the Shadow Factories on the city's outskirts fared better, and astonishingly production was up and running again a mere 5 days after the attack). The people of Coventry, emerging to such desolate scenes, were bereft. Newspapers at the time reported streams of refugees leaving the city over the following days, particularly those residents who no longer felt safe remaining there at night, for fear the bombers might return. Compared to the devastation visited on the populations of other cities such as London, Dresden or Hiroshima, the death toll from the Coventry Blitz may not seem huge, but in the context of a town and the size of Coventry the effect was devastating. The intensity of the raid, both in the percentage of the urban population it affected and the proportion of the city damaged, had an unprecedented impact on the city's population, described by one observer as being in a state of "unprecedented dislocation and depression". The damage was so extensive that the Germans coined a new term after the city to describe the total annihilation of a place—"Koventrieren", or "to Coventrate".

Fig.2-2 A wrecked bus stands among a scene of devastation in the centre of Coventry after the major Luftwaffe air raid on the night of 14/15th November 1940

Fig.2-3 Bomb damage in Broadgate, central Coventry, the morning after the German air raid on the night of 14th November 1940

A Cathedral "Ruined and Rebuilt"

The emblematic site of destruction on that fateful night was without a doubt the Cathedral of St Michael, one of the jewels of the city's mediaeval centre. The Cathedral, with its flat roof and extensive wooden structure, was at high risk during the bombing raids. As such, precautionary steps had been put in place to protect the church and its contents. At the start of the war some of its most precious stained glass windows were removed and stored elsewhere in the countryside. Fire fighting equipment was moved into the Cathedral and placed in strategic points to aid quick use in case of an emergency. A rota of four volunteer fire fighters to keep watch over the Cathedral at night was established, although this proved difficult to keep fully manned. However, these steps were no match for the fire power brought to bear on the city that night. Provost Richard Howard was the Dean of the Cathedral at the time and—as we shall see later in later chapters—a man who would play a key role in Coventry's peace history. Present on the night of the raid, he recorded his efforts to save the Cathedral with a small group of local men in evocative terms:

On the night of November 14th, the Cathedral roof was slippery and shone white under our feet, for there was frost and the bright light of the full moon was reflected on the lead. The guard for that night consisted of Mr. Forbes, aged sixty-five, myself, fifty-six, and two young men in their early twenties. Shortly after we had assembled at seven o'clock, the sirens sounded; and in little more than five minutes we heard the raiders overhead.

Soon the bombs started, and the horizon was ringed with a huge semicircle of light, showing the scores of incendiaries had fallen. More and more were showered down, nearer and nearer the Cathedral. Within a minute of igniting, they exploded with a loud report. Then, towards eight o'clock, the first of the incendiaries struck the Cathedral.

Provost Howard went on to recount their efforts to protect the Cathedral—smothering incendiary bombs in sand and water and putting out fires as they sprung up across the building's roof and inside. By 9:30 pm firefighters from Solihull arrived to assist in efforts to save at least some parts of the building, but their work proved fruitless as the water supply failed and any chance to put out the fires now raging in the Cathedral slipped away. As Provost Howard noted: "At the failure of the water, we realised with some consternation and horror that nothing could now save the roofs of the Cathedral nor any of the interior woodwork, which was already on fire over a wide area." It was not the heavy bombs that proved fatal to the ancient structure of the Cathedral, but the incendiaries, which became lodged on the building's flat roof and set fire to its wooden beams. After only a couple of hours of bombardment, there was little to do but try to salvage some of the contents of the Cathedral, and await the end of the bombing. Provost Howard watched from the porch of a nearby police station as "all night long the city burned, and her Cathedral burned with her".

Fig.2-4 The ruins of Coventry Cathedral two days after the German Luftwaffe air raid on the city on the night of 14th November 1940

The news of the blitz on Coventry was flashed round the world by radio next day. The Government considered it right to release the story of the all-night bombing of the civilian population, of the hundreds of lives lost, of the great damage to homes and factories, and of the destruction of the Cathedral. As the hours went on, and the courageous and cheerful spirit of the people of Coventry became known, "Coventry" sprang into fame as a world wide symbol of the sacrifices which the peoples of the free world would have to endure before victory could be won, and of the spirit in which those sufferings would be endured.

A number of explanations have been offered to explain precisely why Coventry was targeted with such firepower on the night of 14th November 1940. To be sure, it was an important target by virtue of its factories, a key element of the British war economy, as discussed above. This alone would make it a tempting target to an enemy seeking to disrupt the production of aircraft and other items vital to the war effort. However, it has also been suggested that the attack on Coventry was also an attempt to sap the morale of the British public. The beautiful historic centre of the "city of three spires" was well known in the UK, a jewel of mediaeval England. Destroying this heritage would strike a symbolic blow against the history and identity of the United Kingdom, and take revenge against the RAF who—according to one historian—had angered Hitler by bombing historic Munich some days earlier.

This idea is given some credence by the words of German radio the following day, which reported the devastation of Coventry by warning "German thoroughness used to be a byword abroad. It is true we do not like half measures, particularly when we are taking revenge. For British blockade, German blockade; for Munich, Coventry". What is certainly true, is that the raids had an immediately devastating effect on both morale and industry. In the immediate aftermath of the bombing almost three quarters of the city's factories had been seriously damaged. What is more, the effect on Coventry's residents was catastrophic. In the words of one anthropologist, while visiting the city immediately after the raids, "The overwhelmingly dominant feeling was utter helplessness. The tremendous impact of the previous night had left people practically speechless in many cases". The victims of the raids were buried in a mass grave, located in the London Road Cemetery, with the first of several burial ceremonies held on 20th November 1940.

Coventry was to face a number of other deadly raids before the end of the war, notably in April 1941 when 281 people were killed in another sustained raid lasting 7.5 hours. 34 people, including patients, nurses and doctors, were killed when the Coventry and Warwickshire Hospital was hit, and another of the city's once vaunted "three spires", Christ Church, was destroyed, having somehow survived the Blitz the previous November.

Fig.2-5 Coventry after the Blitz, the city houses suffered serious damage

Reconstruction and Rebirth

The immediate response to the bombing was complex. The weeks that followed the bombing were characterised by a mixture of calls for peace and calls for revenge. There was an undeniable tension between the urgent need to return to "business as usual" by restarting the city's factories, and the impossibility of returning to normality in a city where thousands of people had been made homeless. Meanwhile, the city's basic infrastructure lay in ruins. Important dignitaries such as Prime Minister Winston Churchill visited Coventry in the days following the attack to examine the damage, and express their solidarity with residents. Most notably King George VI arrived in Coventry on 16th November, just two days after the attack, to tour affected sites and meet with city officials. The King met residents in temporary shelters and canteens, visited a damaged residential area and toured the ruined Cathedral, to the surprise of Provost Howard, who had not been informed of the King's visit. Reports at the time praised the impact of the King's visit on morale in the city. As Taylor noted, the images of the King in the ruined streets of Coventry were also of great value to the UK's propaganda efforts, particularly in the United States.

Fig.2-6 Prime Minister Winston Churchill inspecting the ruins of Coventry Cathedral

On the same day as the King's visit, *The Times* newspaper used the evocative phrase "A Martyred City" to describe the bombed-out Coventry. This phrase was taken up again in Pathe's footage issued on 21st November, which showed scenes of devastation from Coventry, ruins still smouldering, along with footage of the King's visit. The tone of this coverage is striking: "Words are hopelessly inadequate to describe the horror and indignation all over the civilised world at this wanton devastation", intones the stern narrator, before signing off with the promise of revenge "An eye for an eye, a tooth for a tooth". Immediate responses to the bombing, particularly in the media eager to bolster national morale and attract American sympathy, focused squarely on revenge against the Germans. These reactions did not, notably, talk of peace, reconciliation or forgiveness. At the same time, however, a remarkably different response was also beginning to emerge, centred around the Cathedral. The role of the Cathedral in encouraging a culture of peace and reconciliation in Coventry will be explored in greater detail in Chapter Three. However, it is useful to introduce its first steps here, in the context of the devastation, confusion and anger that characterised the aftermath of the bombing. On the day after the bombing, the Cathedral's stonemason, Jock Forbes, recovered two burnt beams that had fallen from the roof and tied them together in the shape of a cross. Later, someone wrote the words "Father Forgive" above the makeshift cross, creating an altar from the remains of the Cathedral, and centring the notion of forgiveness in this shattered space. Rigby and Valliere describe Provost Howard's next actions as an act of "moral courage befitting one in his position". Given the opportunity to make the Christmas Day national radio broadcast from the ruins of the Cathedral, Howard used this national platform to call for peace and forgiveness, exhorting the listening public:

> *What we want to tell the world is this, that with Christ born again in our hearts today, we are trying, hard as it may be, to banish all thoughts of revenge. We are bracing ourselves to finish this tremendous job of saving the world from tyranny and cruelty. We are going to try and make a kinder, simpler, a more Christ-child like sort of world in the days beyond this strife.*

Eight decades on from the events of 14th November 1940, peace activists in the city today are unanimous in their appreciation of Provost Howard's courage and foresight in making space for peace and forgiveness even in the aftermath of such terrible destruction, and the belief that this decision would have a lasting impact on the identity of the city.

World War II had taken its toll on the city; in addition to the events of 14th November, further bombing raids meant that by the time peace was declared more than a thousand people had been killed in the city, and many thousands more injured. As Gould J. and Gould C. note, "About 800 shops, over 100 factories and 150 other commercial buildings were destroyed, 23,500 houses destroyed or badly damaged and 53 acres (21 hectares) of the city centre devastated". Conversely, Coventry's central role as one of the most important manufacturing centres for armaments and aircraft parts in particular had cemented its place as a powerhouse of manufacturing, and looked set to ensure the city's prosperity in the post-war era. There is, of course, a tension between this centrality of arms manufacturing to the success of the city, and the call for the city to lead a turn to peace and reconciliation, spearheaded by the Cathedral and—as we shall see in later chapters—the City Council. This apparent contradiction at the heart of the city would continue to be a source of tension and subject of intense debate for many years to come.

Given the extent of the damage to the city centre, Coventry's reconstruction was remarkably swift. This was aided by the fact that an extensive regeneration plan for the city had been developed before war had even broken out. As discussed in the previous chapter, the city had retained its mediaeval heart. Whilst the aesthetic and historical value of this was unquestionable, on a practical level it posed a number of problems to Coventry, with its rapidly swelling population and the dawning era of the car. As such, a city architect, Donald Gibson, had been appointed in 1939 in charge of developing a plan for a new city centre. These initial plans were presented to the public just months before the blitz, in May 1940. They actually proposed clearing much of the mediaeval centre that surrounded the Cathedral and central shopping streets, in favour of the construction of low-level civic buildings set in parkland, broad streets, and new modern shopping centres. In this respect, then, it is ironic that much of the damage to the city's architectural heritage brought about by the Luftwaffe bombing was likely to have occurred anyway at the hands of the city planners in peacetime. Certainly Gibson, addressing the Royal Society of Arts in London in December 1940, recognised that "in one night the site is largely cleared and ready for this regeneration".

Fig.2-7 "Father Forgive" altar in Coventry Cathedral ruins

Full plans for the reconstruction of Coventry were presented in 1945, and announced to the public in an exhibition entitled "The Coventry of the Future", and work on the large reconstruction began as early as June 1946. It was, of course, imperative to move quickly. By 1946, 12,000 city residents were waiting for housing. In 1948 the then Princess Elizabeth visited Coventry to lay the foundation stone of the first building in the new city centre, and within a decade most of this initial reconstruction had been completed (although further large-scale construction work to modernise the city and accommodate its rapidly expanding population would take place for many more years). In 1952 Queen Elizabeth returned to Coventry to lay the foundation stone of the new Cathedral, a strikingly modern building which became a symbol of the city's recovery by the time it was consecrated a decade later. As we shall see in the following chapter, the Cathedral has also been a symbol of Coventry's commitment to peace and reconciliation, born out of its wartime experiences. Along with the City Council and civil society organisations, it has been a driving force in making Coventry a city of peace. How and why this has happened in the wake of such terrible violence will be explored over the next few chapters.

Fig.2-8 Coventry city center after the reestablishment

Chapter 3

Coventry's Peace Story:
The Beginnings

There are a number of lenses we can use to understand Coventry's journey from the despair of November 1940 to its rebirth as a city of peace and reconciliation. A chronological view would set out the major milestones in Coventry's peace story as the city has traversed eight decades of major change—locally, nationally and globally—and ask how the city's commitment to peace has helped or hindered it in defining a role and identity in modern Britain. We could also seek to understand this story by looking in greater depth at the main actors involved in Coventry's peace narrative— the Cathedral, the City Council and civil society groups. These three have all played a vital role in working for peace and reconciliation in Coventry, though their motivations, methods and resources have often differed quite wildly, and they have all assumed prominence at various times in Coventry's recent history. A third way of viewing this story could be through the different ways the notion of peace and reconciliation have been viewed in the city since 1940, and the kind of peace that has been talked about. This, as we shall see, has ranged from peace and reconciliation with Germany, to discussions of nuclear disarmament, to questions of racism and inequality within Coventry. Peace, and activities to promote it, have been seen at various times and by various actors as local and global, interpersonal and international, and inspired by religious belief, political philosophy or humanitarian principles.

It is this very complexity—the mixture of actors, motivations, perceptions and time periods—that makes Coventry's story so interesting, and that helps to explain the longevity of the peace narrative in the city. As one former Lord Mayor, interviewed for this book, explained, the range in activities and groups engaged in working for peace in Coventry meant that there was always someone willing "to keep the candle burning" for peace.

This chapter will look in more detail at some of these activities, actors and key moments in Coventry's peace history, to understand how this flame of peace has been kept alive over the years. It will explore Coventry's path since the end of World War II, and particularly how the thread of the peace narrative has run through this, by focussing on a number of key moments, movements and events that have been central to the challenge of building a peace narrative in Coventry. These include the rebirth of Coventry Cathedral as a centre of reconciliation; the development on city twinning initiatives; and anti-nuclear activism and protests against the arms trade. The following sections will demonstrate how the city's initial focus for peace work, from the end of the war up until the mid 1960s, was aimed at reconciling with its enemies in World War II (notably Germany) and joining with other "martyred" cities in preventing future violence. As we shall see, two institutions were crucial in this phase—the Cathedral and City Council, with citizens' groups becoming more influential as time went on.

**Phoenix from the Flames:
Coventry Cathedral's Rebirth as a Centre for Peace and Reconciliation**

One of the most astonishing things about Coventry's experience is how quickly the discussion turned to peace and reconciliation at the end of the war. This can, to a large extent, be attributed to the actions of what one local peace researcher and activist has termed "moral entrepreneurs", that is, individuals with particular influence and status to set the tone of public debate in the aftermath, and mark the city's course towards peace.

Fig.3-1 The ruins of Coventry Cathedral today

Principal among these was the Cathedral and, as already seen in the previous chapter, Provost Howard. In an echo of his Christmas Day broadcast in 1940, Provost Howard was again invited to broadcast to the nation (and further abroad to the Empire, as it was at the time), on Christmas Day 1946. This time, he invited a German counterpart, Pastor Mecklenburg from Hamburg, to join him. As a major port city, Hamburg had been terribly affected by bombing in the war. The exchange between the two clergymen was powerful and striking in its commitment to remaking a new, peaceful relationship between people.

Provost Howard began, stating "You know what happened to us here in Coventry, and you can easily picture what it was like. We know what happened to you in Hamburg, and can partly imagine it…". He went on to suggest two words he wished to share with his counterpart in Hamburg—"Forgiveness" and "New Birth", and explain "Here in Coventry we have 20,000 homes to build, a whole new city centre and a Cathedral to restore. Your task is even greater. But more important still, there is a new spirit to be born—new courage, new faith, new unselfishness, new pity for each other's sufferings, new family love and purity".

The response from Pastor Mecklenburg was a sobering reminder of the destruction suffered by both sides during the war. "I hear your voice, my brother of Coventry", he replied, "and thank you for your Christian understanding. The ruins of Hamburg lie all around me, mile after mile of desolation. Fifty percent of our houses are destroyed and half the remainder damaged… the struggle for existence here is desperate".

Responding to Provost Howard's call for forgiveness, Pastor Mecklenburg also called for peace. "Your message of forgiveness and new birth awakens an echo in my heart. 'Forgive us our trespasses as we forgive them that trespass against us.' If only those words could be echoed in all hearts! If only we could cast out bitterness and hatred and begin again, then I believe that our children—yours and ours—may live together in peace and brotherhood".

From these roots, the Cathedral became both a powerful symbol and actor in the city's work for peace. Indeed, its reconstruction was not only a symbol of rebirth, of new life following the horrors of war, but became a tool for forging new relationships with German communities who, not so long ago, had been seen as bitter enemies.

These first steps in rebuilding relationships with counterparts in Germany were followed in 1947 by an initial visit by representatives of Coventry Cathedral and the City Council to the German city of Kiel. Kiel was in many ways quite like Coventry—a naval base with a highly important shipbuilding industry, the city had also been heavily bombed during World War II, and was particularly targeted by virtue of its role in the war economy (particularly its production of the much feared U-boats). This similarity was, in fact, noted by a British serviceman from Coventry named Gwillym Williams, who had been stationed in Kiel after the war to work on reconstruction. Mr Williams was so struck by the shared experience of the two cities, and he suggested a link between the two be made. Writing in a local newspaper at the time, the Mayor of Kiel Andreas Gayk noted Mr Williams, "This man had immediately done everything in his power to help a town which had shared the fate of his native city", supporting the idea of a link between Coventry and Kiel so that "the names of our ravished cities can become the symbol of our spiritual and moral reawakening".

This hope was soon to become a reality. In 1947 Provost Howard, accompanied by the Mayor of Coventry George Briggs, and trades union representative Wilfred Spencer, visited Kiel and was welcomed by their counterparts. This, as we shall see later in the chapter, was to be the first of Coventry's twinned cities, an important civic peace initiative pioneered in the city. The visit to Kiel also saw the beginning of another programme for peace which was closely identified with the Cathedral. During the visit to Kiel, Provost Howard presented a cross made out of the mediaeval nails that had been salvaged

The Community of the Cross of Nails

Taking its name from the emblematic crosses made from the remains of Coventry's war-ravaged Cathedral, and presented to churches and other organisations with the exhortation to work for peace from the late 1940s, the Community of the Cross of Nails (CCN) today counts more than 200 active members in 45 countries. As a Christian organisation, all the community's members share a common goal of working for reconciliation, whether this is at the personal, local or international level. Whilst many CCN members are churches, they also count educational organisations and charities amongst their number. Members are guided by the three principles of the Community of the Cross of Nails: Healing the wounds of history, Learning to live with difference and celebrate diversity, and Building a culture of peace. Recently the Cathedral launched a sister organisation to the CCN called "Together for Hope", which aims to bring together organisations working for the same aims of peace and reconciliation from different, or no religious backgrounds.

from the Cathedral's ruined roof to the St Nikolai Church, as a symbol of peace and renewal. In return, Provost Howard was given a stone from one of the churches destroyed in the bombing raids. The stone now sits in the Cathedral's Chapel of Unity, where it is known as the Kiel Stone of Forgiveness. The cross of nails would become a powerful symbol of reconciliation, presented by the Cathedral to more than 200 churches, charities and other centres across the world.

Over the coming years, the Cathedral continued to work with their counterparts in Germany to host symbolic events that would underline the commonalities between two places so recently divided by war, and underline their commitment to reconciliation. For example, when the Honorary Canon of Brandenburg, Adolf Kurtz, visited the Cathedral in 1950, Provost Howard asked him to deliver a service in German in the Chapel of Unity. One of Provost Howard's most enduring contributions to promoting a culture of peace and reconciliation through the Cathedral, was the introduction of the Litany of Reconciliation, written by Canon Joseph Poole in 1958. This short prayer repeatedly echoes the words "Father Forgive" inscribed by Provost Howard on the Cathedral wall the morning after the bombing raids. To this day, the litany is recited everyday at noon in Coventry Cathedral, and in its ruins every Friday. The litany is also spoken in members of the Community of the Cross of Nails, particularly those churches that have also experienced great trauma. At the reconstructed Frauenkirche in Dresden, for example, the litany is repeated every Friday, serving as a "weekly timecheck for our reconciliation activity", according to one church official.

Fig.3-2 Coventry Cathedral gave the Cross of Nails to Kiel as a gift

The Litany of Reconciliation

All have sinned and fallen short of the glory of God.
The hatred which divides nation from nation, race from race, class from class,
Father, forgive.
The covetous desires of people and nations to possess what is not their own,
Father, forgive.
The greed which exploits the work of human hands and lays waste the earth,
Father, forgive.
Our envy of the welfare and happiness of others,
Father, forgive.
Our indifference to the plight of the imprisoned, the homeless, the refugee,
Father, forgive.
The lust which dishonours the bodies of men, women and children,
Father, forgive.
The pride which leads us to trust in ourselves and not in God,
Father, forgive.
Be kind to one another, tender-hearted, forgiving one another, as God in Christ forgave you.

By the end of 1958, Provost Howard handed over the reins of the Cathedral to a new leader, but one who was just as committed to the institution's growing mission of peace and reconciliation, Bill Williams. As Goebel notes, just weeks after taking up his new position at Coventry, "Williams travelled to Berlin to promote Anglo-German friendship. On his arrival at the airport he held aloft a cross of nails and said 'As you made Coventry a symbol of destruction, so now, join with us and make it a symbol of reconciliation'".

Rebuilding for Peace—The Reconstruction of Coventry Cathedral

The reconstruction of the Cathedral also represented a powerful opportunity to make a statement about Coventry's commitment to peace and reconciliation. At the end of the war, much of Coventry's city centre still lay in ruins, and nowhere was more striking than this in the skeletal remains of the burned-out Cathedral. There was a clear need to reconstruct, and quickly. For the rest of the city centre, this was taken as an opportunity to modernise the city centre by Coventry City Council, especially its pioneering city architect Donald Gibson. Gibson sought to introduce new planning principles to Coventry, characterised by modernist architectural ideas and first presented to the public in a landmark exhibition in 1940 entitled "The Coventry of Tomorrow".

The attitude to the Cathedral was markedly different, however, at least in the beginning. As early as 1943, Provost Howard had appointed the highly respected English architect Sir Giles Gilbert Scott as the architect for the reconstruction of the Cathedral. Scott was already well-known for designing Liverpool Cathedral and the monumental Battersea power station in London. However, the choice of Scott was not popular within the church—whilst some expressed concerns that a Catholic would not know how to design a Protestant place of worship, others were disappointed that the designs were too traditional, rebuilding the ruined Cathedral at least in part and reprising many of its stylistic features. Faced with these criticisms, Scott withdrew from the project.

These concerns reflected a debate that had been raging since the Cathedral's destruction—and one that continues today in many sites that have been destroyed by war or disaster. Is it better to try and reconstruct exactly what stood before the crisis hit, maintaining historical accuracy, or to rebuild something new, something which reflects the difficult experiences of the place and the needs of the communities that surround it? This is a question faced by many places emerging from conflict, from the cities of World War II, to contemporary cases such as the war-torn cities of Iraq and Syria. In Coventry, opinion was similarly divided. As Farnell explains, the City Council Planning Committee believed "the Cathedral should be rebuilt in stone on its old site, an exact replica of the medieval church of St Michael", whereas Alderman George Hodgkinson, the Committee's vice-chairman at this stage, observed that there was "a growing feeling among the citizens that the ruins ought to be retained as a monument to man's indiscretions between 1939 and 1945". In many ways, Coventry pioneered a new approach to this challenge, as we shall see below.

As work began to rebuild Coventry after the end of the war, the question of how to remake the Cathedral became more pressing. As a result, in 1951 the Cathedral's Reconstruction Committee launched a design competition for proposals for a new cathedral. This competition was intended to do more than just rebuild a place of worship—the Committee hoped the winning design would "capture the imagination of a new generation of church-goers and provide a powerful focus for the public spaces of the city". The competition received 219 entries, which varied greatly in their architectural style and treatment of the ruins of the old Cathedral. Whereas some envisioned a reconstruction that fully incorporated the ruins into the structure of the new building, the winning design, submitted by Basil Spence, preserved the ruins as they stood alongside a strikingly modern new building.

Spence's design stands in startling contrast to the ruins next door, and purposefully so. As the architect himself explained, "The shell of the building which survived has inspired millions of visitors by its eloquent and fragile beauty. The new Cathedral grows out of the old. The porch links the two buildings—as the ruins stand for the Sacrifice, so the new Cathedral speaks of the Resurrection". When touring the site today, representatives of the Cathedral's reconciliation ministry liken the move from the ruins of the old Cathedral to the splendour of the new as reflecting the journey from the pain and sorrow of conflict, to the hope of peace and forgiveness. The porch, they stress, shows how the two experiences are linked. From the ruins you can look forward to the promise of the new Cathedral, and the possibility of peace, whilst from the new Cathedral the reminder of the conflict and its terrible consequences are also always visible through the vast etched glass west window. The new Cathedral's design also features a chapel dedicated to peace and reconciliation—the Chapel of Unity. This space is richly decorated with mosaics and stained glass, representing reconciliation between faiths and nations.

Fig.3-3 The old and new Cathedrals seen side by side

Fig.3-4 The aerial view of Coventry Cathedral under construction

Fig.3-5 The stained glass windows in the new Cathedral building

Fig.3-6 Detail of the new Cathedral, featuring Jacob Epstein's sculpture of St Michael and the Devil by the front steps

It is not just the design of the new Cathedral which contributed to the city's message of peace and reconciliation, however. Throughout the period of its reconstruction, a number of gifts of labour, money and artefacts were made to the Cathedral as symbolic gestures towards peace and forgiveness. For example, when the German President Dr Theodor Heuss made a state visit to the UK in 1958, he brought a donation of 50,000 marks to contribute to the construction of the Chapel of Unity, which he presented to Provost Howard. This was not universally welcomed at the time, as passions against Germany still ran high in post-war Britain. One UK newspaper reported the German government's contribution as "blood money", and criticised the Cathedral for accepting it. The baptismal font is carved from a boulder from outside Bethlehem, donated by the government of Jordan as a gesture towards cooperation among the Christian, Islamic and Jewish faiths. It was carved, like the stone tablets that line the walls, by Ralph Beyer, a German mason living in the UK, whose Jewish mother was killed in Auschwitz.

Perhaps the most powerful contribution to rebuilding the Cathedral in the name of peace was made by the involvement of young German volunteers in the rehabilitation of the ruined Cathedral's vestries. The West German organisation Aktion Sühnezeichen Friedensdienste (Action Reconciliation Service for Peace) started working with the Cathedral in 1960. A team of young people came to Coventry to live and work for six months, restoring the vestries so that they could be used as an international centre for reconciliation. As former Canon of Coventry Cathedral Paul Oestreicher notes, "two volunteers staffed the International Centre for many years, ran a soup kitchen for the less-privileged and for passing tourists, and told their stories", continuing the reach of this extraordinary act of restitution.

In return, a group of young people from Coventry visited the city of Dresden to engage in a similar act of restitution. This was no easy task, since by the early 1960s political tensions were running high between the UK and East German governments, where Dresden was located. Indeed, the very act of reaching out to counterparts in East Germany was at times difficult for the Cathedral's partners in West Germany also, as Rose notes, "there was a period when Kiel found it difficult to accept that Coventry was seeking reconciliation also with Dresden in the German Democratic Republic". After a number of years of sensitive negotiations, in 1965 the first party of volunteers from Coventry was able to travel to Dresden to work alongside German volunteers in rebuilding the Deaconess Hospital. Volunteers from Coventry would work for six months to move five tons of rubble by hand and clean 25,000 bricks for reuse in rebuilding the hospital. Volunteers from both sides described the deeply moving experience of working to restore the physical fabric of cities previously seen as enemies, and this remains a powerful example of practical restitution and reconciliation following conflict.

By 1962, Coventry's new Cathedral had completed construction and was consecrated, including the opening of its new international centre for reconciliation, thanks to the hard work of these German volunteers.

Civic Leadership—Coventry City Council and the Pursuit of Peace

Extraordinary as it was, it is doubtful that Coventry Cathedral's commitment to peace and reconciliation would have had the same impact (or at least, an impact outside those within its faith community) had it not found an equally willing and committed partner in the pursuit of peace and reconciliation in the City Council. Described by one local peace activist as "old fashioned socialists" with a commitment to international solidarity, the Labour-led City Council of the post-war years pursued a number of activities and policies that further reinforced the city's turn towards a politics of peace and reconciliation rather than revenge.

Having assumed control of the Council in 1937, just two years before the outbreak of war, the Council now had the perfect chance not only to demonstrate the benefits of municipal socialism in the city, but also to show that international solidarity based on this politics could lead to peace. Indeed, the long-standing Coventry MP Richard Crossman would later remark as much when reflecting on the city's post-war experiences and the achievements of another key figure in the local Labour movement, George Hodgkinson. Hodgkinson was a long-standing city councillor and Mayor of Coventry from 1944 to 1945, who was at the heart of many of the city's civic peace-building initiatives.

The Birth of City Twinning

In fact, the Council's work in this regard began before the end of the war. In November 1941, a year after the Coventry Blitz, the local Labour Party founded the Coventry Anglo-Soviet Unity Committee. Coventry was not alone in setting up such a body, which aimed to raise funds for suffering Soviet cities and promote support for the wartime Anglo-Soviet alliance. However, for a city still reeling from its own experiences of conflict, this was all the more poignant. Coventry's contributions were mainly sent to the city of Stalingrad (now Volgograd), soon to be the site of one of history's most terrible battles. Along with medical supplies, the women of Coventry sent a message of friendship to the women of Stalingrad, with a book signed by 6,000 local women. The message read "from this city, scarred and ravaged by the enemy of civilisation, our hearts go out to you, who now face slaughter and suffering even more fearful". This was later followed by another gesture in response to the horror of the Battle of Stalingrad, when around 900 Coventry women embroidered their names on a tablecloth along with a message of sympathy, and sent it to Stalingrad.

Fig.3-7 The signature book of thanks by Stalingrad women given to Coventry women

By 1944, the City Council formalised these links by creating the Coventry-Stalingrad Bond of Friendship Committee. However, there would be no visit by an official delegation from Stalingrad until some time later, in 1951. As with the case of the Cathedral's outreach in Dresden, there existed at times a tension between the civic engagement being pursued in Coventry and the political relationships at the national and international levels. In this case, the wartime alliance between the UK and USSR broke down swiftly at the end of World War II, and at times hindered the city's outreach to cities such as Stalingrad.

The link with Stalingrad was not the only one pursued by the City Council. In the years that followed the end of the war, the Council organised visits to and from a number of European cities that had also suffered badly during the war. In addition to the historic visit to Kiel discussed above, in 1947 delegations from the Council visited Prague and Lidice, then in Czechoslovakia (now the Czech Republic). The village of Lidice was another emblematic site of the horrors of World War II, where the entire village was destroyed and around 340 civilian inhabitants killed in an act of revenge by Nazi soldiers in 1942. In 1952 a delegation visited Belgrade (modern-day Serbia, though part of Yugoslavia then). Then, a visit was returned the following year when the Ambassador of Yugoslavia came to Coventry and offered a gift of timber from the city of Belgrade to aid the construction of a new theatre in the city. The following year, a delegation from Coventry visited Stalingrad, and took the opportunity to launch an appeal to the United Nations against weapons of mass destruction.

As these visits grew in number and frequency, they gave rise to a powerful tool in promoting peace and reconciliation which would be pioneered by Coventry, and led by the Council—city twinning. There had been instances of twinning or partnership agreements between towns or cities before (notably the West Yorkshire town of Keighley is often identified as the earliest twinned town for its link with Poix-du-Nord, France). However, Coventry was the first city to systematically pursue a policy of formalised links between cities, including visits by official delegations and, eventually, ordinary citizens, as a means to building peaceful relationships and mutual understanding. Starting with the "Bond of Friendship" with Stalingrad in 1944, and agreements with Kiel and Lidice in 1947, the pace of city twinning increased in the 1950s, when Coventry formed links with a number of cities in Europe and further afield. Many of these cities (such as Caen, Warsaw, Dresden, Arnhem or Belgrade) had undergone significant damage during the war, which contributed to the logic of twinning with Coventry.

Later twin towns (largely post-1960) were often chosen for cultural or economic reasons. Given the political tensions between East and West Europe at the time, it is striking that so many of Coventry's early partners in twinning were found behind the so-called "Iron Curtain". This is a testament to both the leadership of Coventry's left-wing council, who were more able to reach out to these countries than might otherwise be possible, and to their commitment to using twinning to support peaceful relations and increase mutual understanding. Although as Tiratsoo notes, this was not without its critics at the time, and may have contributed to the Labour

Party losing several seats on local council in 1955. It shows that sometimes cities have the leeway to act independently of national policy in pursuing these kinds of policies—as we shall see below, this was not the only time Coventry City Council's approach diverged from that of the national government when it came to matters of peace and conflict. The Council's leadership in this matter was recognised at the European level in 1955, when the city was awarded the Council of Europe European Prize. The application submitted by the Council to the prize committee has underlined the city's role in taking "the leading part in the development of friendly relations and understanding with their counterparts in other European countries".

Coventry's Twin Towns

1944 Stalingrad (Russia)
1947 Kiel (Germany), Lidice (Czech Republic)
1955 St Etienne (France)
1956 Parkes (Australia)
1957 Caen (France), Belgrade (Serbia), Graz (Austria), Sarajevo (Bosnia and Herzegovina), Warsaw (Poland)
1958 Arnhem (Netherlands), Cork (Eire)
1959 Dresden (Germany), Ostrava (Czech Republic)
1960 Bologna (Italy)
1962 Coventry (Connecticut, USA), Dunaujvaros (Hungary), Galati (Romania), Kecskemet (Hungary), Kingston (Jamaica)
1963 Granby (Canada), Windsor (Canada)
1971 Coventry (Rhode Island, USA)
1972 Cornwall (Canada), Coventry (New York, USA)
1983 Jinan (China)

Fig.3-8 Detail of Coventry city street view

Coventry's Civil Defence Controversy

Another instance in which the City Council departed from national policy, and which contributed to the formation of Coventry's identity as a city of peace, was the "civil defence controversy" of 1954. This episode in the city's history is amply covered in Nicholas Barnett's article "No protection against the H-bomb: press and popular reactions to the Coventry civil defence controversy, 1954". This controversy erupted in the city in the wake of massively powerful testing of nuclear weapons by the United States at Bikini Atoll, known as the Castle Bravo test. The extent of this test, and its aftermath, heightened anxiety in the UK over the possible impacts of nuclear war. In this atmosphere, Coventry City Council took the decision not to implement its civil defence requirements—that is, not to recruit and train a Civil Defence Corps which would be mobilised to carry out rescue and relief work in case of a national emergency such as nuclear attack. This, the Council reasoned, was pointless in the face of the overwhelming and devastating scale of a nuclear attack—there was, quite simply, "no protection against the H-bomb".

The Council's refusal to participate in civil defence commitments electrified public debate around the use and impact of nuclear weapons, both at a local and national level. When a civil defence exercise took place in the city in late May, members of the Council joined antinuclear protestors to oppose it. Council members were subject to a great deal of hostility from the media and public during the controversy, particularly painting them as being in the pay of Russia. However, as Barnett notes, it seems likely that their stance played an important part in swaying public opinion about nuclear weapons. Whereas at the start of this period opinion polls from April 1954 showed that 52% of the public believed nuclear weapons made war less likely, by May 1954 61% of people surveyed "believed a nuclear war would destroy civilisation". In this way the Council's actions can be understood to have contributed to the burgeoning anti-nuclear movement, which was to take off more fully with the founding of the Campaign for Nuclear Disarmament (CND) just three years later.

A Conference for Peace

Of course, whilst the City Council may have had some success in taking a stand on nuclear warfare within the city, this was of little consequence to the continued ratcheting up of pressure on the international stage. By the early 1960s tensions seemed to be reaching a boiling point in the eyes of Coventry Mayor William Callow, who continued to be gravely concerned by the prospect of a Third World War. Callow decided to hold a peace conference, reaching out to the leaders of other cities with the following declaration released on 15th August 1961:

> *Sixteen years ago today the Second World War came to an end. Today we stand in a position of unparalleled danger. At such a moment we, the undersigned leaders in the City of Coventry, a city which suffered grievously from the effects of mass bombing, appeal to the citizens of the world. We would bring before you [four] points.*
>
> *1. First, the value of personal contact. We appeal to the citizens of our city and the world to make two decisions. First, they will not hurl abuse from a distance at those with whom they disagree and, secondly, that they will not indulge in the trigger-happy attitude that war is inevitable and that the sooner we get down to it the better. Such ideas and statements are contagious and can do nothing but harm.*

2. Let us face the fact that in East and West the leaders and the ordinary people are being driven by fear. Fear is always a dangerous mentor. Frank admission of fear by both sides can mark the beginning of the process of healing. This will be accelerated when each of us does his utmost to understand one another's reasons for fear.

3. We believe there is a profound difference between appeasement and reconciliation. Appeasement takes the form, "Peace at all costs regardless of the rights of others in order that our own rights may be preserved". But reconciliation is only achieved through costly honesty and painful adjustment, having full regard to the rights of others and with slender regard for our own rights.

4. We call upon the ordinary men and women to recognise the power of prayer. Prayer is not a last resort of the frightened but a first line of attack for the realist. In this connection the leaders of the Churches of this city are arranging a day of "Prayer for Peace" to be held in Coventry on Sunday next, the 20th August.

Arising out of this appeal, the Lord Mayor proposes to call together the lord mayors and mayors of all the cities with which Coventry has bonds of friendship. To this end he is issuing an invitation to them today.

Signed: William Callow (Lord Mayor)
  G. E. Hodgkinson
  Cuthbert Coventry
  A. H. Jones
  L. J. Davey
  T. L. K. Locksley
  W. H. Edwards
  Simon Phipps
  D. Fairburn
  S. Stringer
  F. Green
  R. Walsh
  S. Verney
  A. J. Waugh

This appeal shows how the city sought to actively mobilise its growing twinning network in a practical support for peace. What is more, the signatories to the statement are noteworthy. They not only represent members of the Council but also trades unions, cooperatives, and the Anglican, Catholic and nonconformist churches of Coventry, demonstrating the broad appeal of this position, and the power of these institutions working in common cause. Central to the appeal is a clear statement from the civic authorities of the link between Coventry's wartime suffering and peacetime aspirations, one that mirrors the message emerging from the Cathedral at the same time. The Conference accordingly took place on 26th September 1961, bringing delegates from across the world (but particularly from Coventry's twinned cities) to the city. Interestingly, however, there was little participation from other UK cities.

At the end of the conference, the Mayors of Coventry, Stalingrad, Lidice, Graz, St Etienne, Parkes, Warsaw, Aosta and Caen signed another "Appeal to the Mayors and People of Towns throughout the World". This document stressed the dangers of the nuclear arms race, advocated "universal disarmament" and praised the value of people-to-people contact and the role of cities in promoting peace and reconciliation. As Kaczka-Valliere reflects, it is not clear that this conference had great impact on changing policy in the wider world, but for Coventry it was another important step in cementing its commitment to international friendship, and its identity as a city of peace and reconciliation.

1962 onwards—The Growing Role of Civil Society

Up until the early 1960s, much of the responsibility for Coventry's turn to peace had been in the hands of the Cathedral and Council, as we have seen. However, from 1962 onwards a third pillar of support began to emerge, one that would be crucial for the continued development of the city's peace narrative for the coming decades. This was the increasing involvement of citizens' groups in initiatives to support and promote peace and reconciliation.

Probably the most significant early example of this was through the founding of the Coventry Committee for International Understanding (CCIU). This body was supported by the City Council, which envisioned that it would be a kind of citizens' counterpart to its own twinning activities. The CCIU would work "to encourage friendship with people abroad, organising exchange systems and links with Coventry's twin towns". In the early days of the Council's outreach and twinning initiatives, visits had been undertaken by officials from civic, political and religious institutions. The time was now right, it was felt, to broaden participation in these kinds of activities to include ordinary Coventrians—what Rigby and Kaczka-Valliere termed "Cold War peacemakers". Councillor and former Mayor George Hodgkinson explained the creation of the CCIU as natural response of "Citizens who had personal experience of the horror of war, who had felt the heat and fire of bombardment from the air and been involved willy-nilly as targets in the bestial business of killing and being killed" and were concerned at the international political climate of the time, "which harboured all the elements and threats of a Third World War". The mission of the CCIU was immediately quite popular—by 1966, just 4 years after it had been formed, the Committee had 85 members, each representing a different organisation or network in the city.

In practice, the CCIU worked closely with the City Council (particularly its International Friendship Committee) to facilitate the involvement of citizens' groups in visits to Coventry's partner cities. This support was often invaluable when faced with the complexities of travelling to countries behind The Iron Curtain, particularly at a time when international travel was not the norm for the vast majority of ordinary people. For example, the CCIU was active in facilitating exchanges between Coventry and the German cities of Kiel and Dresden, supporting school groups, youth orchestras, teachers and women's groups to make these trips and learn more about each other. In many ways, this growing involvement of ordinary citizens in writing and shaping Coventry's peace story sets the scene well for its development over the following decades, as the immediate impact of World War II receded in the city and the mission of peace and reconciliation found new ways of being expressed and relevance with new generations of Coventrians.

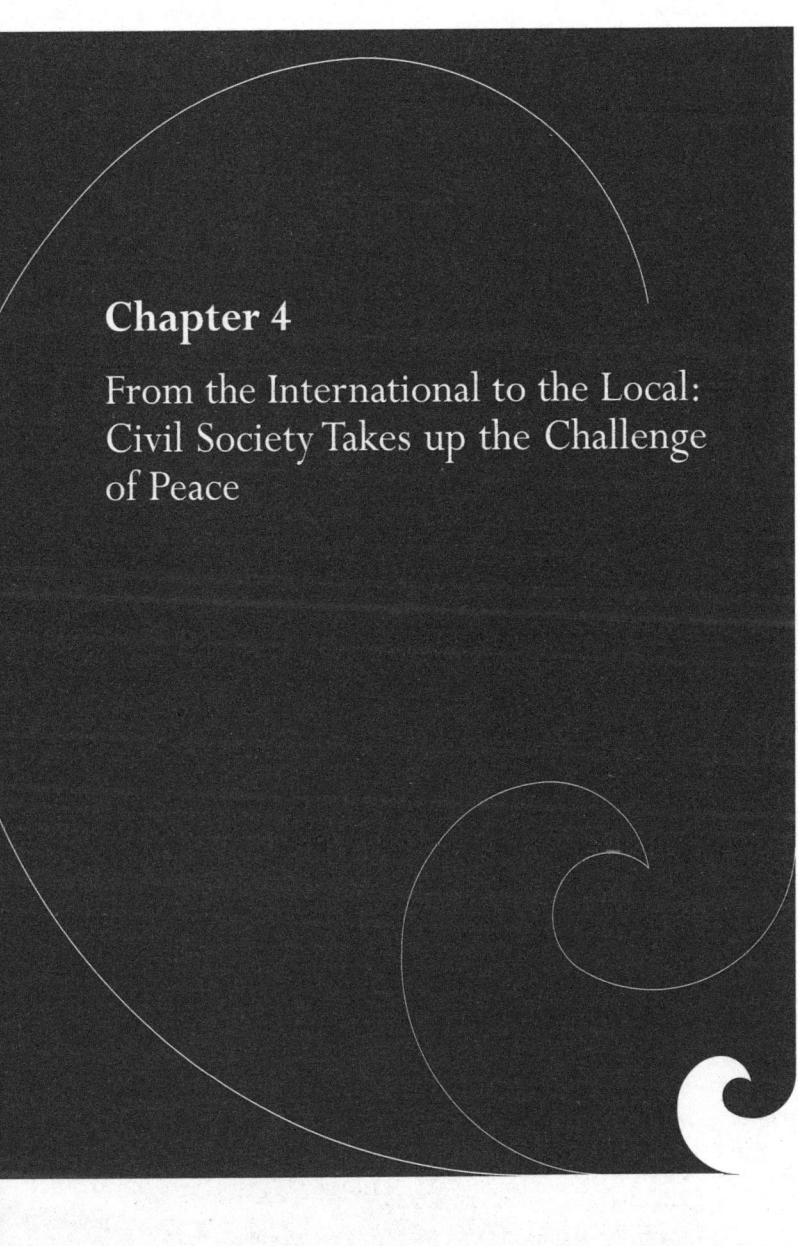

Chapter 4

From the International to the Local: Civil Society Takes up the Challenge of Peace

As we saw in the previous Chapter, the initial flowering of Coventry's mission of peace and reconciliation was successful because it had the support of two powerful institutions in the city, the Cathedral and the City Council. By the 1960s, a third pillar in Coventry's peace identity began to emerge—the work of civil society. This chapter will trace the emergence and evolution of civil society's engagement in peace work in the city, from the early days of the Coventry Committee for International Understanding (CCIU) to the development of a broad range of civil society initiatives and organisations in the 1990s. It will also examine how the industrial decline faced by the city from the 1970s challenged the peace narrative, and how this was in many ways revitalised by its association with the anti-racism campaigns that emerged in the 1980s.

People-to-people Peace—The Coventry Committee for International Understanding

Whilst there had been some initial involvement of citizens in peace and reconciliation initiatives in Coventry (for example, through the messages of support from the women of Coventry to the women of Stalingrad), the first systematic attempt to engage individual citizens in Coventry's peace work was through the establishment of the Coventry Committee for International Understanding (CCIU) in 1962. Councillor Hodgkinson, again at the heart of this initiative, saw CCIU's founders as people who felt a personal responsibility for building peace, as they had lived through personal and direct experiences of the horrors of war during Coventry's bombing, as unwitting participants in "the bestial business of killing and being killed", and who therefore felt a personal responsibility to do what they could as individuals to prevent future conflict of the kind they had witnessed in Coventry.

The aim of the CCIU was "to encourage friendship with people abroad, organising exchange systems and links with Coventry's twin towns". This body worked hand in hand with the Council—in fact it was set up under their auspices—and sought to complement the activities of the Council's city twinning committee by promoting the engagement of ordinary people in visits and exchanges with twinned cities. Previously such visits had largely been the domain of municipal officials or, to a certain extent, between school parties. As Rigby and Kaczka-Valliere report, the establishment of the CCIU was met with enthusiasm. Kaczka-Valliere has observed elsewhere that at the heart of the CCIU's popularity lay a strict commitment to remaining politically non-partisan, which enabled it to attract a wide group of participating organisations from across most (but not all) of the political spectrum.

The CCIU remained close to the Council, receiving some funding from it from 1967 onwards. The organisation played an important role in encouraging and helping to organise international travels at a time when this was less common and potentially quite daunting for many local people. As well as helping Coventrians to travel abroad, the CCIU also helped to find hosts for incoming visitors from the twinned cities. In addition to its core activities to facilitate visits between Coventry's citizens and their counterparts in other countries, the CCIU also organised events and meetings for local people interested in peace. For example, from 1967 the Committee organised an annual public lecture, in memory of one of its founding members Alderman Callow. One notable speaker to be invited was the Nobel Prize winner and former Coventry MP Philip Noel-Baker. The CCIU also organised social gatherings to try and encourage friendship between the city's different communities, particularly as immigration to Coventry grew during its post-war boom. However, these meetings were never as successful as the CCIU's core work in support of widening participation in city twinning.

By the 1980s, however, the work of the CCIU had decreased markedly. This can be linked to the overall context of industrial decline witnessed in Coventry over this period (discussed in greater detail below). Social change and the rise of mass tourism also meant that the Committee no longer needed to play the role of pseudo travel agent. In the light of this changing role, the CCIU decided to rename itself as the Coventry Association for International Friendship (CAIF) in 1998. The CAIF maintains close links with the Council and a focus on the twinned cities, organising events in Coventry that celebrate these relationships, welcoming visitors to the city and participating in visits, particularly to the city's German counterparts.

Acorns for Peace—John and Yoko

On the occasion of the People and Cities conference, John Lennon and Yoko Ono visited Coventry in order to contribute a piece of art for peace to a sculpture exhibition taking place at the Cathedral. At the height of their international fame and embarking on a high-profile campaign of peace activism, they planted two acorns facing east and west inside a circular wrought iron bench that they situated near the Cathedral. The intention of the piece, named "Acorns for Peace", was to celebrate the peaceful meeting of the East and West. Unfortunately, John and Yoko met with a frosty welcome from the Cathedral, who disapproved of their unmarried state (or rather, that they were both married to other people). Worse, both acorns were stolen a few days later, following which Lennon organised for the bench to be removed. Years later, in 2005, the city invited Yoko back to replant two new acorns in the Cathedral's Unity Gardens, along with a replica of the original bench, in a ceremony with local school children.

Throughout this period the Cathedral maintained its commitment to working for peace. From 1964 onwards, it had a full-time education department, dedicated to working with local schools in particular to spread Coventry's message of reconciliation. In 1968, it hosted a peace conference entitled "People and Cities" which would perhaps be best remembered for the impromptu intervention by former Beatle John Lennon and his partner Yoko Ono (see box). Throughout the 1970s, the Cathedral also started to expand the horizons of its peace work beyond the former foes of World War II to other conflicts. Indeed, in 1975, Provost Williams wrote of the focus on reconciliation with Germany—"That phase of my work is now ended and a new theme for our work in Germany and Europe today is required... Your present attention to Europe's responsibility for the Third World must be the dominant theme for the next phase".

In 1973, the Cathedral appointed its first International Director, Canon Kenyon Wright, to oversee this work. Canon Wright had previously spent many years running an urban ministry in Calcutta (India), and was passionate about expanding the Cathedral's work on reconciliation, peace and justice to a wider audience. Throughout the 1970s, links were made with institutions and communities working for peace in Northern Ireland, the Republic of Ireland, Israel and India, whilst the Community of the Cross of Nails continued to expand.

Industrial Decline and the End of the Golden Age for Peace?

After the trials of the war years, the 1950s and early 1960s could be considered boom years for Coventry. The city became the second largest car manufacturer in the world, home to famous names such as Daimler and Jaguar. This was, in the words of one historian, "a workers' city", where the average wage was around 25% higher than the national wage at the time, and unemployment rates often fell below 1%. The city had risen from the horrors of war, with a modern new city centre, thriving industry and confident population to prove it. This confidence can perhaps be seen in the way the city went about pursuing the goal of peace, and the resources it was able to marshal in support of this work. However, it is important to ask whether all of the city's residents have shared in this post-war dividend of peace and prosperity. Was Coventry a peaceful city for everyone who lived there?

The economy of the 1950s and 1960s had, in Coventry as in the rest of the UK, been buoyed by the arrival of large numbers of immigrants from Commonwealth countries, in particular South Asia and the Caribbean. The city's factories needed labourers to keep up with their expansion, and large numbers of people came to the city to work and secure a better future for their families. Of course, in this regard they were merely following in the footsteps of many who had come to Coventry to contribute to its industry and economy since the Industrial Revolution. Whether these newer residents of the city experienced it as a place of peace and reconciliation is far less clear.

Caribbean and South Asian residents in the city often faced serious discrimination in the city, from poor working conditions to segregation in the workplace and public spaces such as pubs or social centres, lower wages, and in the worst cases racist attacks. Self-help associations such as the Indian Workers Association (IWA) sprung up to try and protect minority communities and fight for their civil rights to be recognised. One IWA member later recalled the struggle for equal opportunities for workers from Commonwealth countries, saying "there were many factories (in Coventry) that would not employ black workers. We would struggle against this discrimination, like on Harnall Street, there was GEC, and they would not employ Indian workers". The discrimination and injustices faced by these Coventry residents challenge the city's right to call itself a city of peace and reconciliation in this golden age. What good, one might ask, is it to seek good relations and understanding with people in Volgograd or Kiel, when a whole section of Coventry's own residents was at the same time being oppressed and denied their equal rights? As we shall see, this question would become more acute following the city's unfortunate—and dramatic—industrial decline.

Across the UK, the economic picture had begun to decline towards the end of the 1960s. The comparative stagnation of the British economy (when seen against its European contemporaries) along with the widespread deindustrialisation, began to take its toll on the cities of the UK. Coventry was no exception. Whilst the strength of its automotive industry may have delayed the impact of deindustrialisation in Coventry somewhat, it could not hold back the tide. By the 1970s, factories were shedding employees and the city was entering a period of sudden decline. As Farnell notes:

> Between 1975 and 1982 these companies removed 55,000 jobs from their books in Coventry. The boom city of the 30 post-war years became the clinically depressed city of the next 20. From their highest point in 1966, employment levels in the city had fallen 18% by 1978. Coventry's workforce was highly specialised and dependent on the manufacturing industries—as these declined, so did the city, shedding 46% of its jobs.

The impact on the city and its residents was harsh, and presented a real challenge to the city's commitment to its identity as a peace city. One of the best-known images of Coventry in the industrial decline comes from a local band, The Specials, whose hit song *Ghost Town* paints a picture of the frustrations and emptiness of the once proud city. The Specials were formed in Coventry in 1977 and became one of the most popular Two Tone bands in the country. Their music fused influences from Ska—a music genre from Jamaica—with punk and new wave music from the UK. The Specials (along with another Coventry-based Two Tone band The Selecter) were distinguished by their multi-ethnic line-up—rare at the time—and their commitment to engaging with political issues, particularly the anti-racism movement. As Beider reflects, "From the outset, Two Tone both brought together and balanced these different traditions, rooted in working-class culture and taking place in a city that was in the grip of an unprecedented economic decline. The genre promoted black-and-white-chequered designs that, while branding an aesthetic, emphasised the importance of embracing multiculturalism and addressing racism". The Two Tone movement was more than a musical subculture and a pop sensation. A mixture of social, economic, political, cultural and local material affected the way the bands formed, the image they developed, and the music they performed. The young Coventry musicians thus developed Two Tone by borrowing from their surroundings, then expressing their experiences. In short, a wide variety of environmental influences shaped, defined and was reflected in the Two Tone movement.

Ghost Town paints a poignant picture of Coventry, and one that seems far from the notion of a city of peace and reconciliation, with fighting amongst youths and an angry population. In fact, the song was to be the soundtrack to a summer of riots in the UK, with racial tensions, urban deprivation and accusations of police brutality spilling into violence in Brixton, Birmingham, Liverpool and Leeds. Whilst Coventry was untouched by rioting, two acts of racist violence were to spark protests in the city. Protests which would, eventually, bring a new relevance to Coventry's peace identity.

Ghost Town
>The Specials

This town (town) is coming like a ghost town
All the clubs have been closed down
This place (town) is coming like a ghost town
Bands won't play no more
Too much fighting on the dance floor

Do you remember the good old days before the ghost town?
We danced and sang, and the music played in a de boomtown

This town (town) is coming like a ghost town
Why must the youth fight against themselves?
Government leaving the youth on the shelf
This place (town) is coming like a ghost town

No job to be found in this country
Can't go on no more
The people getting angry

This town is coming like a ghost town
This town is coming like a ghost town
This town is coming like a ghost town
This town is coming like a ghost town

Jerry Dammers

Confronting Racism—The Fight for Peace Begins at Home

Although, as discussed above, discrimination on the basis of ethnicity had long been a painful feature for Coventry's black and Asian communities, this was further sharpened in the context of the city's perilous decline. In 1981 two events occurred that shook the city to its core and kick-started the growth of the anti-racism movement in the city. On the 18th of April 1981, racist Skinheads attacked 21-year-old Sikh student Satnam Singh Gill, stabbing him to death in broad daylight. The murder caused consternation amongst Coventry residents, and particularly those from minority groups. A march against racism was organised by the newly-formed Coventry Committee Against Racism (now Coventry Against Racism), a broad coalition of organisations from community groups to religious and political bodies.

On 23rd May, over 8,000 people joined the "March for Racial Harmony". They marched from Foleshill, where Singh Gill had been killed, to the city centre calling for an end to racism. Whilst it began as a peaceful protest, the march was met by Skinheads and members of the far-right National Front as they approached the city centre, leading to skirmishes between the marchers and their attackers, many of whom gave Nazi salutes. By the end of the day, 74 people had been arrested. Worse, just a couple of weeks later on 7th June, a popular local doctor, Dr Amal Dharry, was attacked and killed in another racist attack in the Earlsdon area of the city. Once again, this was met by protest by local groups, who organised a concert against racism featuring local bands—notably The Specials—on 22nd June.

Years later, interviewed for this book, numerous prominent local peace activists recalled that it had been the events of 1981, the terrible murders of Satnam Singh Gill and Amal Dharry, that had first led to their involvement in peace work in the city. These tragic events, and the response of communities in Coventry, spurred a new group of Coventrians to become aware of the city's narrative of peace and reconciliation and to use this to support their own work. Crucially, this also gave the city's peace identity a new relevance to people who had not been directly affected by the events of 1941, either because they were too young or had not lived in the city at the time.

Linking the struggle against racism to the wider work for peace re-energised the peace narrative at a time when engagement with this had declined, particularly from the municipal angle, and gave the activists access to a network of resources to support their work. It also began to address one of the long-standing tensions at the heart of the city's peace narrative—that work for reconciliation at the international level was not matched at the local level, where discrimination remained a serious problem. The early 1980s marked a turning point, or perhaps a second phase, in Coventry's experience as a peace city. Whilst many activities retained a focus on promoting international peace and security, increasing efforts to build peace between communities in Coventry itself began to draw on this narrative also. It is from this moment that the third pillar supporting the city's peace work—civil society—really began to come into its own.

The Rise of Civil Society Peace Activists

The number and type of organisations that have emerged from civil society since the 1980s to work for peace in Coventry is large and highly varied. These have ranged from tiny (even one person) campaigns to large-scale events that have become part of the city's annual calendar. The causes they address have encompassed everything from anti-racism, the rights of refugees and migrants, environmental protection, poverty, animal rights, anti-nuclear or arms trade campaigns, disability rights and much more. Such a breadth of focus itself demonstrates how the idea of "peace", and what Coventry as a city of peace and reconciliation should stand for, and has been interpreted in an increasingly broad manner as the years have progressed. The following sections will focus on just a few of these initiatives to give an overview of how civil society groups in Coventry have taken up the mantle of working for peace and made it their own.

Coventry Peace House

The tension between Coventry's identity as a peace city, and its long-standing role in the arms industry, has long been a source of concern for some of the city's most committed advocates of peace. As a place that has actively claimed the title "city of peace and reconciliation" it also actively participate in the production of weapons of war, has repeatedly been highlighted as a serious contradiction at the heart of Coventry's approach to peace.

This tension came to the fore, for example, in 1984, when around 10,000 people marched through the city in support of the Campaign for Nuclear Disarmament (CND). Indeed, the debate still rages today. The Campaign Against the Arms Trade estimates that there are seven companies currently operating in Coventry with links to arms manufacturing, and local activists have been pursuing a sustained campaign calling for the Council to change its pension fund for employees, since the current fund invests in weapons manufacturing. However, as students of conflict transformation will know, these kinds of debates and conflicts can also generate opportunities and ideas for new action. Such is the case for one of Coventry's enduring civil society peace initiatives, the Coventry Peace House.

The Peace House has its roots in a campaign against arms manufacturing in Coventry. From June 1997 until July 1998, a small group of activists had set up a peace camp at the gates of the Alvis factory in Coventry. They were protesting the company's role in manufacturing arms, and specifically in selling tanks to a regime in Indonesia. After around a year of protesting at the factory and raising awareness of their work through letters to the press and engagement with local politicians, several of the group decided to work to establish a more permanent presence for peace in the city.

By 1999, they had bought a small row of terraced houses in the city centre, which they renovated and reopened as the Coventry Peace House. The Peace House served a number of purposes. It was a communal living community for like-minded people seeking to live in a peace-focused community. It served as the initial home of the Coventry Refugee and Migrant Centre and continues to host a night shelter for asylum seekers. From 2003, it established an education trust with the aim of running projects related to environment protection and social inclusion. The following year it began to run a bike workshop to promote sustainable transport in the city. Above all, the Peace House maintains a highly local focus, and a commitment to engage with some of the city's most marginalised communities.

In the words of the Peace House itself— the house represents "community, visitors, friends, ideas, discussions, anti-capitalism, anti-militarism, campaigning, creative solutions, writing, demonstrations, consensus, non-violence, warm fires, cooperation, empowerment, environmental work, cycling, bike fixing, challenging oppression, laughter, tears, eating together, gardening, vegetables, flowers, DIY, maintenance, art, music…". This vivid description once again underlines how Coventry's peace narrative has been broadened through the engagement of civil society groups.

The Lord Mayor's Committee for Peace and Reconciliation

Another important civil society body promoting the city's peace narrative is the Lord Mayor's Committee for Peace and Reconciliation. This committee, made up of around 20 individuals drawn from different bodies and organisations across the city, started off life more closely aligned to the Council. Formed in the early 1980s, it was envisaged as a working group to support the organisation of a peace festival to commemorate the 40th anniversary of the Coventry Blitz. In its early days, it would not have been accurate to characterise the Committee as a civil society initiative—it was chaired by the Lord Mayor, with the Cathedral taking a leading role in coordinating events. However, over the years that followed, the voice of civil society organisations in the Committee became stronger. By the time the Committee was formally established in 1987, the balance of power had shifted. Whilst the Committee retained its links with the Lord Mayor, it had begun to operate independently. Indeed, as Kaczka-Valliere notes, the privileged relationship the Committee retained with the office of the Lord Mayor, as well as the prestige denoted by the use of this name in their title, have probably enabled the Committee to have a greater impact and to "speak truth to power".

Throughout the 1980s, the Committee was responsible for organising the city's Peace Festival. This annual event was a diverse affair and made particular attempts to link challenges to peace and reconciliation at the international level to what was going on in Coventry at the local level. Typical activities included "a range of social, cultural and educational events—special theatre productions on peace themes, a peace run, twin town photo exhibitions, peace education workshops, peace painting competitions and the like". The Peace Festival ceased to be held after 1990—although it has since been revived and represents an important event in the city's calendar today—but the Committee's work had by then expanded to take on a number of other important roles and events. These included convening an annual public peace lecture, held in the Cathedral on the anniversary of the city's bombing. The lecture has attracted a variety of well-known speakers, who have addressed the question of peace from a range of angles. These have included former Prime Ministers and other politicians (Harold Wilson in 1983, Edward Heath in 1993, and Dr Mo Mowlam—famous for her role in the Northern Ireland peace process—in 1998), campaigners (Bruce Kent, from the Campaign for Nuclear Disarmament, 2001), authors (Michael Morpurgo, author of the acclaimed children's book *Warhorse* in 2016, and Yasmin Alibhai-Brown in 2018), and religious figures (Dr Zaki Badawi and Sir Sigmund Sternberg in 1999, and Canon Paul Oestreicher in 2017).

The Committee has also organised an annual commemoration for Hiroshima Day since 1987. This is usually held in the Chapel of Unity, although it is designed as a ceremony for people of any or no faith. Through a mixture of readings, silences and the ringing of the peace bell, participants remember those who lost their lives in the bombing of Hiroshima and Nagasaki.

A third initiative undertaken by the Committee has been the development of a "Peace Trail"—a walking tour around the different sites in the city centre associated with Coventry's history of peace and reconciliation. The trail takes in 31 places in the city, beginning with the ruins of the Cathedral and taking in key places that help to tell Coventry's peace story, from statues and memorials, to trees, buildings, and streets or squares. It finishes at Millennium Place which, as we shall see in Chapter Five, represents another phase in Coventry's attempts to understand how its rich peace heritage can remain relevant to the city as it continues to grow and change.

The Positive Images Festival

Another important event in Coventry's calendar of peace-focused events and another example of how civil society organisations have taken on a leadership role in this work, is the Positive Images Festival. Established in 1995, this arts festival seeks to celebrate the city's heritage, traditions and diversity, presenting a more positive view of the city than the stereotypical image of industrial decline and urban blight that had come to predominate since the 1980s. For three weeks every June, the festival "celebrates the people of Coventry" through a programme of events—spanning theatre, visual arts, literature, dance and music, with a particular focus on events that celebrate Coventry's diverse multicultural communities. Many of these events are directly linked to the city's peace identity. For example, the 2017 edition of the festival produced a book of poetry by local people entitled "War and Peace", and for the past 20 years the festival has incorporated events for Refugee Week.

More widely, however, the Positive Images Festival can be understood as another example of the successful way that Coventry's peace narrative has been turned inwards onto the city itself. The 1980s and 1990s can perhaps be understood as a turning point in the city's understanding of peace and reconciliation. From this point, and particularly through the engagement of a wide variety of committed and passionate local activists, peace has been understood as not just something to be pursued internationally, in response to the horrors of World War II or fears of the Cold War, but something to be achieved at the local level, between and through the people who call Coventry home.

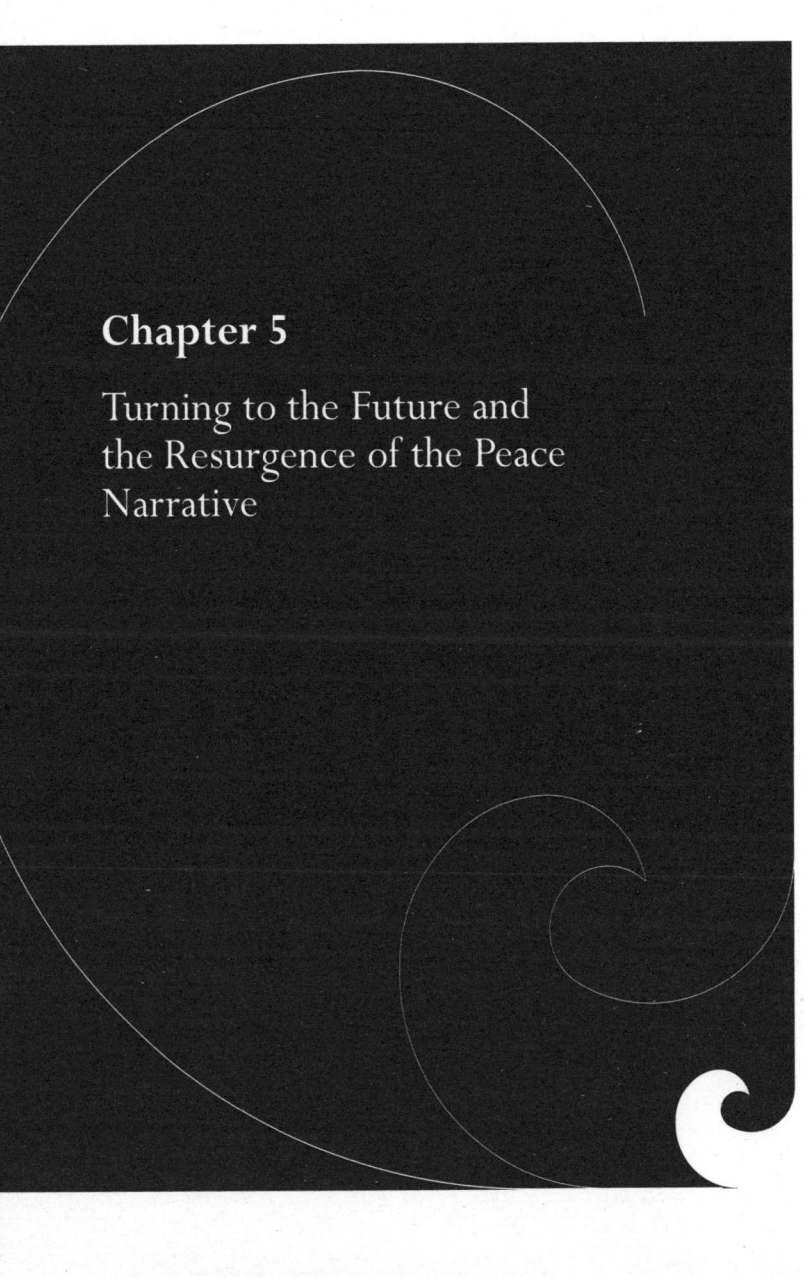

Chapter 5

Turning to the Future and the Resurgence of the Peace Narrative

By the turn of the century, the three pillars that have sustained Coventry's peace narrative since the darkest days of World War II would seem to be in place. The Cathedral, the City Council and civil society organisations had all carved out a distinctive way of working on peace and reconciliation, with each bringing a new perspective to these issues, whether taking inspiration from Christian beliefs, seeking to extend the ideals of international solidarity or turning a critical lens of peace back onto relationships within the city. The harsh economic realities of the late 1970s and 1980s had challenged the peace narrative. From the perspective of the municipal authorities, it had become hard to justify spending time and money pursuing initiatives such as twinning at a time when unemployment at home seemed to be inexorably increasing. For many living in the city, particularly those from minority groups, the kind of discrimination and abuse they faced in daily life undermined the city's claim to peacefulness. And yet, by the late 1990s, the city's commitment to peace was seemingly re-energised, buoyed by the engagement of a new generation of activists and residents. These groups linked the narrative of peace and reconciliation to a wider range of issues than ever before; from environmental activism, to work with asylum seekers and refugees, from initiatives to address urban poverty to festivals celebrating Coventry's unique and diverse identity. As the city approached the new millennium, the idea of peace was assuming a renewed centrality in Coventry's identity at the local, national and international level.

The renewed importance of Coventry's peace identity can be witnessed through a number of key developments in the city in the 2000s, which will be explored in greater detail below. These include the increasing scope of the Cathedral's interventions to support peace on the international stage; the establishment of a centre for peace and reconciliation studies at Coventry University; and an ambitious urban regeneration programme for the city centre, which placed the city's peace identity at its very heart. However, as we shall see, the renewed importance of the city's peace narrative has not been without its criticisms, with some observers questioning whether this amounts to little more than a city "branding" opportunity rather than a root and branch adoption of peaceful principles.

Coventry Cathedral's International Ministry—A Proactive Force on the International Stage

Coventry's renewed confidence in its peace identity was reflected in the assurance with which the Cathedral's International Ministry including the International Centre for Reconciliation pursued a unique and highly proactive approach to peacemaking at the international level. Under the direction first of Canon Paul Oestreicher (from 1995), then Canon Andrew White (from 1998), the Cathedral built on its reputation as a centre for peace and reconciliation by actively engaging in conflict mediation in a number of high-profile cases, offering its good offices to support negotiations for peace. The words of Canon White reflect this mission, and particularly the sense that the Cathedral had a responsibility to engage with contemporary conflicts. He later reflected on his time at Coventry saying "When I took over the Reconciliation Centre I said, 'we've got to deal with the issues of today. The biggest issue is going to be how we relate to Islam… the biggest political situation is going to be Iraq and Israel/Palestine'. So, I started going there". In particular, the International Ministry focused on cases where the specifically religious nature of the Cathedral as an institution would help its message to resonate with the actors concerned, or enable greater access to the conflicting parties.

In effect, this renewed international commitment translated into the Cathedral's involvement in a number of high-profile negotiations and mediations, largely centred on the involvement of other religious institutions. In January 2002 Canon White, acting with the support of the Cathedral, brought together a group of high-ranking religious leaders from the Christian, Jewish and Muslim communities in Israel and Palestine. Meeting in Alexandria (Egypt), the aim was to bring together these religious leaders to discuss prospects for peace and demonstrate high-level leadership in support of dialogue and reconciliation. This was no small task, and despite a great deal of prior groundwork, the negotiations at the conference proved highly challenging, with each delegation required to face difficult political concessions. However, it was eventually successful, and the Alexandria Declaration of the Religious Leaders of the Holy Land was signed to great acclaim (and with the assent of then Palestinian and Israeli leaders Yasser Arafat and Ariel Sharon) in January 2002. Whilst the impact of this declaration may, in hindsight, not have lived up to the high expectations of the time, it remains a striking example of the Cathedral's willingness to use its unique position to try to intervene in contemporary conflicts.

Fig.5-1 Peace posters were placed in the Cathedral

This model was reproduced later in the year, in northern Nigeria. This region had been plagued by inter-religious conflict between Christian and Muslim communities—riots in the year 2000 had claimed the lives of around 2,000 people, and violent inter-communal tensions continued to be a problem for communities in and around Kaduna. Using the Alexandria Declaration as a model, the Cathedral helped to convene a group of respected religious leaders in Kaduna to develop a declaration in support of peace and dialogue, which was signed in August 2002. However, this too would be tested by further violence following the country's hosting of the Miss World beauty pageant in 2002, which resulted in another 250 deaths.

Perhaps one of the most successful examples of the Cathedral's role as a trusted mediator, and one that is testament to the personal profile of Canon White in the Middle East region, came in April and May 2002. Here Canon White played a key role as the mediator of negotiations to end the siege of the Church of the Nativity in Bethlehem. The siege had come about when a number of Palestinian militants had fled from the Israeli Defence Force operation and sought sanctuary in the Church, one of the holiest sites in Christianity, alongside over 200 monks and Palestinian civilians. The church was surrounded by IDF soldiers demanding the surrender of the militants inside. Canon White's reputation as an interlocutor trusted by both sides, with the backing of a respected institution, meant he was requested to oversee negotiations to end the siege. He eventually spent 39 days negotiating the safe release of the monks, civilians and militants (although sadly a total of 8 people lost their lives during the siege).

Whilst these examples demonstrate the international reach and ambition, it is important to also recognise that at the local level the Cathedral continued to play a vital role in supporting the peace narrative. In particular, the education programme instituted in the earliest days of the peace mission had gone from strength to strength. In 1989, it was estimated that 10,000 school children visited the Cathedral to learn about its commitment to peace and reconciliation every year. By 2011 this number had risen again to 14,000 per year. From 1996 onwards, this thriving educational programme for young people was mirrored by the development of a centre for the study of peace within Coventry University, as we shall see below.

Establishing an Academic Centre for Peace in Coventry

When it was opened in 1996, the Centre for the Study of Forgiveness and Reconciliation (CSFR) at Coventry University represented another important step in ensuring the city's focus on peace continued. Today, this centre (now called the Centre for Trust, Peace and Social Relations) is one of the largest of its kind, and its establishment towards the end of the 1990s was another sign that institutions in the city recognised the value of Coventry's peace narrative. In its early days, the Centre attracted some prestigious speakers to the city to reflect on their experiences of peace and reconciliation, such as the Irish President Mary Robinson in 1996, and former South African President F. W. de Klerk in 1997.

However, it was in 1999 with the arrival of Professor Andrew Rigby as the director of the Centre that it began to really develop as a hub for education and research. Professor Rigby identified the potential "niche" of a Coventry-based research centre as a focus on peacebuilding, non-violent conflict transformation and reconciliation, all directly linked to the city's historic peace mission. This would enable the centre to stand out from other academic centres that focused on areas such as security studies, international relations, war studies or international development.

Fig.5-2 Centre for Trust, Peace and Social Relations of Coventry University

As we shall see throughout this chapter, this reflected a wider realisation throughout the city during this period that Coventry's historic association with peace and reconciliation gave it a unique identity and one that could be used to differentiate, even market, the city and its institutions on the national and international stage.

From 1999, the Centre began to develop on two fronts, with a growing research agenda related to peace and reconciliation on the one hand, and the establishment of formal educational programmes on the other. In the year 2000, it offered an MA in Peace and Reconciliation Studies for the first time, which was followed by a pioneering online Certificate in Peace and Reconciliation in 2003. By 2007 (and having changed its name to the Centre for Peace and Reconciliation Studies in 2005), the Centre counted 70 students across three courses and had developed a burgeoning research community of 10 PhD students supported by a number of full-time academic staff. The Centre—and by extension the University—had become another important pillar in Coventry's peace community. Like their colleagues in the Cathedral and civil society groups, members of CPRS also tried to maintain a balance between initiatives that focused on peace at the international level (research projects in Israel and Palestine, for example, or the development of new partnerships with academics in Nanjing), and those that engaged with the local context and community (for example, delivering night school classes for local people).

Today, the Centre for Trust, Peace and Social Relations (as it has been known since 2014) has grown into a significant hub for research, teaching and consultancy. It counts over 72 staff, delivers several MA programmes and is home to 55 PhD students. The Centre hosts the Academic Council of the United Nations, and leads large-scale programmes to support peaceful communities in Coventry (such as the MiFriendly Cities initiative aimed at supporting refugees and migrants in the region). It has an international research profile, with researchers working on 83 separate research programmes, covering topics as diverse as United Nations Peacekeeping and maritime security, to international migration, heritage protection in conflict or far-right extremism.

Branding a City of Peace and Reconciliation
—The Council Re-engages

Perhaps the most striking feature of this period in Coventry's peace story was the way in which the City Council re-engaged with the peace narrative, placing it at the heart of regeneration and development initiatives in the city. Following the relative decline of the city in the previous decades, an ambitious regeneration plan for the city centre was launched at the end of the 20th century, representing the largest urban redevelopment of Coventry since the post-war reconstruction. The aim of this project was to reconnect key sites in the city (the Cathedral and the Transport Museum), opening them up to pedestrians and bringing more visitors to the city centre. This ambitious project was called the Phoenix Initiative, drawing on a symbolism (the emergence of new life from the flames of destruction) that had been popularised in the city since its recovery from the war. From the very start, the city's peace identity was a central element of this project. The municipal authorities wanted a design which would:

> *Create a metaphorical journey, and an actual pedestrian route, through the centre of the city with the theme of reconciliation between history and the future. Beginning with the past, represented by the bombed-out shell of the Cathedral, with the new Cathedral rebuilt alongside, the journey would pass through the fringes of the town centre and end near a new Garden of International Friendship, symbolic of the anticipated future.*

Much as the planners and architects working in Coventry in the 1940s and 1950s saw an opportunity to rebuild the city, its flagship buildings and civic spaces in a way that would promote an image of peace and prosperity, the Phoenix Initiative again represented another attempt to integrate a peace identity into the very fabric of the city. The use of public art was central to this. For example, the Garden of International Friendship contained a "maze" designed by a British artist Kate Whiteford, and has poetry composed by David Morley set into its walls. These poems engage with the events of the Coventry Blitz, placing them in the context of the city's long and rich history.

Perhaps the best-known piece of art developed as part of the Phoenix Initiative was the conceptual artist Jochen Gerz's "Future Monument" [Fig.5-3]. Gerz was a German artist who had lived through the allied bombing of Berlin as a child, and he had a marked interest in exploring questions linked to political narrative and public memory through his work. As Vickery reflects in his discussion of the Coventry works, Gerz maintained an interest in understanding "how civic identity emerges through historic narratives of people and events, and how these narratives inform the political discourse of nation statehood. Spaces of 'memorialisation', like city squares with their monuments, function in this way for Gerz".

He designed two pieces for Coventry, with the explicit aim of engaging with the complexities of the city's peace narrative, and particularly its relevance to local residents—the Public Bench [Fig.5-4] and the Future Monument. To Gerz, the participation of local people was vital—he asked them to respond to two questions at the start of the project, "Who are your past enemies? Who are your current friends?" The Public Bench is a long-curved bench that runs around one side of the newly created Millennium Place. Coventry residents were asked to contribute names to be fixed above and around the bench on plaques, similar to those found in many memorial spaces. The names and dates featured on each plaque represent encounters, secret relationships or open friendships that people in Coventry wished to record.

Fig.5-3 A view of Millennium Place, featuring Joachim Gerz's Future Monument and the Whittle Arch

Fig.5-4 A view of Millennium Place, featuring Joachim Gerz's Public Bench

In Millennium Place also stands the Future Monument. This relatively modest glass obelisk, lit from within, is surrounded by glass plaques set into the floor again developed through engagement with the local communities. Eight plaques bear the names of countries most commonly named by residents as former enemies, reading "To our British friends; To our French friends; To our German friends; To our Irish friends; To our Japanese friends; To our Russian friends; To our Spanish friends; To our Turkish friends". A number of other plaques reflect the city's current diversity—any group in the city that could gather 40 signatures could apply for a plaque that recorded their presence in the city.

The centrality of Gerz's works to the Phoenix Initiative demonstrates the willingness on the part of the municipal authorities to place the city's peace narrative at the heart of its public identity. Indeed, Rigby and Kaczka-Valliere demonstrate that a peace identity had been identified by the Council as bringing potential economic benefits to the city, and quote a 2004 position paper produced by the City Council setting out the value of this approach to the city:

> *Promoting peace and reconciliation will have obvious benefits for those people living in areas of conflict, for the citizens of Coventry in terms of educational value and awareness of international issues as well as promoting peace within the city, which contributes to racial harmony and community cohesion. The city's image will also benefit as a result of promoting the peace and reconciliation theme showing the city in a positive light to a global audience.*

Gerz's works, however, also help to remind us of the ever-present tensions in this peace narrative. By insisting on asking city residents to consider enemies as well as friends and engaging with parts of the city that did not fit with the shining vision of the future portrayed in the Phoenix Initiative (Vickery describes him "wandering around council estates and visiting communities, some of which did not register on the radar of the 'public' organs of civic life"), Gerz delivered a more complicated view of peace, reconciliation and its role in Coventry's future. The works are also located next to another monument created as part of the Phoenix Initiative, the Whittle Arch. This striking structure celebrates one of Coventry's most famous sons, Frank Whittle, the inventor of the jet engine. The juxtaposition of friendship gardens, ambiguous monuments to peace, and a tribute to this giant of British aeronautics (and Royal Air Force officer) recalls the uneasy way that the city has balanced its commitments to peace activism and its involvement with the arms industry over the years. In this way the Phoenix Initiative and the renewed involvement of the municipal authorities in promoting the peace narrative, reflect the same tensions that have existed in Coventry's peace identity since the very morning after the Coventry Blitz.

Chapter 6

Looking to the Future

So, what lessons can we learn from Coventry's experiences since that fateful night of November 1940? Arriving in the city by car, visitors cannot fail to notice to road signs proclaiming "Coventry—A City of Peace and Reconciliation", but to what extent can we consider Coventry to be a truly peaceful city? Have the people of Coventry succeeded in learning the lessons of history, as those that stood in the ruins of the Cathedral surely hoped they would? The previous five chapters have presented a brief introduction to the city of Coventry and its peace story, and represented an attempt to begin to discuss some of these questions, if not answer them fully.

The book began by describing the city and its historical development, painting a picture of Coventry as it stood on the eve of World War II. At a time when tradition (in the form of its rich medieval heritage) rubbed shoulders with modernity (represented by the industrial might of the city and its factories), it was these same factories—the source of both pride and wealth in the city—that drew the eye of the German military. Chapter Two described the terrible events of the Coventry Blitz and traced the impact of that fateful night, the devastation it wrought on both the physical and emotional fabric of the city. It also showed how the immediate response to this crisis—particularly led by the Cathedral and supported by the City Council—opened the door to a unique experiment in forgiveness and reconciliation, by using the city's terrible experience of the violence of war to call for peace.

Fig.6-1 Peace sculpture, situated in Coventry's downtown street corner

Chapters Three to Five traced the development of this call for peace over the following decades. They have shown how different actors—the Cathedral, the municipal authorities, civil society organisations and latterly the University—have become involved in supporting, shaping and reproducing the peace narrative in the city. This has ensured that this narrative has always been carried forward in some form even when the interest in it, or the capacity to pursue it, has waned in one or more sectors. These chapters have also demonstrated the malleability of this narrative. The way that the ideas of peace and reconciliation, and what they mean in a city like Coventry, have been interpreted and reinterpreted by different groups over the years, has been a key element of their continued relevance in the city. Peace and reconciliation in Coventry have, over the past seven decades, meant improving relationships with former foes in Germany, and reaching out to communities behind the Iron Curtain. It has meant taking a critical look at relationships within the city and trying to find more peaceful ways of living together in diverse communities (something which has long been part of the Coventry story, given its long history of migration). Peace and reconciliation in Coventry have been interpreted as a religious imperative as well as a socialist one, also as an international affair and a local concern. The notion of being a peaceful city has been understood as a direction to welcome refugees, to protest arms manufacturing and nuclear war, to develop international friendships, and as a unique part of the city's identity, culture and heritage.

Threats to the Peace Narrative

This journey has not been without its tensions and contradictions, however. As we have seen in the preceding chapters, the historical and contemporary relationship between the city's industrial base and the arms industry has been a continual source of tension in Coventry's peace identity. This tension has not subsided in recent years. In 2015, an investigation by a local newspaper revealed that the City Council's pension fund had invested over £50 million in weapons companies. Two of these companies have offices based in the city. This was revealed at the same time as the City Council announced it would be rehoming 78 refugees fleeing the brutal conflict in Syria, as part of its commitment to being a "City of Sanctuary". That many of these firms produced weapons being used in Syria at that moment, was a cruel irony to many in the city. Similarly, another group of local peace activists, the Coventry Justice and Peace Group, has waged a long campaign to convince the same pension fund to stop investing in four companies involved in the manufacture of cluster bombs (a type of bomb so horrific it had been made illegal in the UK in 2010). Their campaign was finally successful in 2017, when it was announced the fund would no longer invest in two of the companies, whilst the other two ceased manufacturing this type of munition.

These debates around the Council's indirect investment in weapons companies demonstrate two important things about the city's relationship to its peace narrative. Firstly, Coventry's relationship to arms manufacturing remains an unresolved issue, a thorn in the side of its claims to be a city of peace and reconciliation. On the other side of the coin, however, these debates also point to the continued existence of lively debate and committed activism in support of peaceful principles in the city. In fact, as we have seen throughout previous chapters, a number of important peace initiatives in the city, such as the Coventry Peace House, have emerged at least in part in opposition to the local arms industry.

The weapons industry is not the only challenge to Coventry's peace claims. One of the most commonly expressed concerns by people interviewed whilst researching this book was whether, after all this time, these ideas of peace and reconciliation actually meant anything to Coventrians in their everyday lives. There is a deep level of introspection amongst those people engaged in peace work in Coventry as to whether or not the city's much-vaunted peace identity is actually helping its citizens to live more peacefully in their daily lives. It is easy to understand where these concerns have arisen simply by glancing through the local press.

Fig.6-2 The Knife Angel during its display in Coventry

In 2016, as the UK debated whether to leave the European Union (an institution which was itself established in order to build peace in a war-ravaged Europe), Coventry voted strongly to leave. This, it must be recalled, was a city that was once awarded a Europe-wide prize for its contributions in building European relations. In the days following the vote, the local media reported xenophobic attacks in the city, a trend that was later backed up at both the local and national levels by police figures. Home Office figures revealed that hate crime spiked nationally in the month following the EU referendum, increasing by 41% compared to the previous year. Whilst this dropped by August, levels remained higher than in the corresponding period in the previous three years. Coventry saw annual-reported hate crimes rise from 377 in 2015 to 404 in 2018, demonstrating a trend about which council leaders expressed grave apprehension. Of equal concern in recent years has been the apparent rise in knife crime in the city, which had nearly doubled in the city in the five years between 2012-2013 and 2017-2018.

The murders by stabbing of a number of young men in the city in recent years have shocked residents. In March 2019, a powerful sculpture was erected temporarily outside the Cathedral to draw attention to the terrible toll being extracted by knife crime, and to pay tribute to those who have been affected by it. The Knife Angel [Fig.6-2] is an eight-metre-high sculpture constructed from 100,000 knives handed into police across the UK. Its symbolic placement by the new Cathedral, and directly in front of Jacob Epstein's famous sculpture of St Michael vanquishing the devil, once again draws the viewers' attention to the ongoing struggle to build peace in Coventry. Although the situation in the city should not be overstated—on the whole Coventry remains a safe place, with an overall crime rate which falls below the national average—these increases in violent acts again challenge the idea that Coventry can be considered a city of peace and reconciliation. It can be of little surprise that local peace activists are concerned about the impact of the city's peace identity, given such worrying rises in hate and knife crimes.

Lessons from Coventry

Do these challenges, then, mean that Coventry's experiment in peace has failed? Should we consider its designation as a city of peace and reconciliation no more than good Public Relations for the city, at best a laudable aim from decades past rather than an accurate description of the present? This seems too harsh a judgement of the city, and the work so many of its residents have dedicated in the pursuit of peaceful ideals. In truth, it is probably fair to say that whilst Coventry may not have achieved the goal of being a truly peaceful city (in fact, we might ask if any place has yet achieved this lofty aim), there is still great value in the steps the city has taken to promote values such as forgiveness, peace and tolerance.

Firstly, the importance and moral leadership shown by people such as Provost Howard and Alderman Hodgkinson in working for reconciliation in the aftermath of terrible tragedy cannot be understated. By reaching out to former enemies and pursuing a variety of practical and often innovative ways of building peaceful relationships with them, Coventry still provides a powerful example of how a city can respond to the experience of violence by working for peace. What we can really learn from Coventry's experience is that peace is possible even when it seems unthinkable, and even when conflicts and tensions are ongoing (for example, during the Cold War). Cities are perhaps uniquely placed to work for this. They occupy a space between the local and the national, bringing together enough political and economic capital to pursue ambitious plans in the name of peace, and the ability to reach out to friends and former foes alike in a different way to national governments.

Secondly, Coventry remains one of the only places where questions of peace and reconciliation form part of the civic discourse, and continues to drive initiatives in the city, even many decades after the end of World War II. This can be seen through the continued engagement of the main institutions that have supported peace work in the city, the pillars of its peace identity—the Cathedral, the City Council and civil society organisations, more recently the University. Rather than losing relevance as the direct memory and experience of the events of the Coventry Blitz have grown more distant in time, the number and variety of initiatives that draw on the peace narrative now seem greater than ever. From peace orchards to peaceful schools initiatives, refugee integration programmes to the annual RISING Global Peace Forum [Fig.6-3], festivals, interfaith forums and in-depth academic research projects, peace remains on the agenda for many people in Coventry and is supported by these pillars. Developing similar structures—different in nature but complementary in their commitment to peace—would seem to be a priority for any other city seeking to develop a peace identity.

Fig.6-3 The scene of "RISING Global Peace Forum 2019"

Thirdly, the continued work of the pillars of peace work in Coventry is not the only thing that has contributed to the longevity of this narrative. From the immediate aftermath of the Blitz, when Jock Forbes created a makeshift cross from the damaged beams of the Cathedral to the civic rebirth of the 1950s, and the regeneration of the late 1990s, Coventry has built its peace city into the bricks and mortar of the city. From the large scale to the small scale, from monumental to everyday spaces, public space in the city centre is full of elements that remind residents of this peace story. So much of the cityscape are pressed into the service of memory for peace. This is not contained by the formal or informal divide, and it doesn't stay within the bounds of the Cathedral, or the Herbert's Peace Gallery, or the offices of the Centre for Trust, Peace and Social Relations. There are street names that commemorate other cities affected by extreme violence, street architecture that shows where houses once stood, peace trees, a peace walk, and the Future Monument. The phoenix imagery throughout the city (included on the University logo) refers to Coventry's resilience from conflict and its brighter future. At the heart of the city, just as it was intended all those years ago, the ruined and rebuilt Cathedral stands as a striking reminder of the city's unconventional response to violence to anyone passing by.

Fig.6-4 Logo of Coventry University

As so many theorists of peace and reconciliation have emphasised, peace is not a fixed end point or a final goal that can be achieved. Rather we should understand it as a process, something that must be constantly worked on and reaffirmed by every generation. Perhaps Coventry's success has been in making sure successive generations of residents for the past eight decades have been able to participate in this process and have had the tools and opportunities to ask "whose peace are we working towards" and "what kind of peace do we want". Certainly this short overview of Coventry's peace history has shown that the answers to these vital questions have changed over the years, as more people have been brought into the conversation and new challenges have presented themselves. As mentioned at the start of this volume, Coventry has been the UK City of Culture in 2021, a designation the City Council is understandably proud of. This year-long event will once again provide an occasion to highlight the unique role peace and reconciliation plays in the city's identity. Projects such as a fourteen-foot-high illuminated peace poem ("Paper Peace", by the artist Robert Montgomery) which has recently been situated at various points in the city, give a glimpse of how this important cultural milestone might celebrate—and challenge—Coventry's peace narrative. It also represents an important chance to draw a new audience into the process of renewing the city's commitment to peace, making this speak in relevant and engaging ways to another generation of Coventry residents and visitors alike.

A hundred years and the dream never ends. All our tomorrows are fragile. The peace builders are heroes of kindness. Peace is a dream of a shared human soul that we build every day with forgiveness and kindness and hope.

"Paper Peace", Robert Montgomery

Main Bibliography

1. Barnett, N., No Protection against the H-bomb: Press and Popular Reactions to the Coventry Civil Defence Controversy, 1954, Cold War History, 2015, 15(3), pp. 277-300.

2. Beider, H., White Working-class Voices: Multiculturalism, Community-building and Change, Bristol: Policy Press, 2015.

3. Campbell, L., Coventry Cathedral: Art and Architecture in Post-War Britain, Oxford: Clarendon Press, 1996.

4. Dubensky, J., Peacemakers in Action: Volume 2: Profiles in Religious Peacebuilding, Cambridge: Cambridge University Press, 2016.

5. Gill, T., The Indian Workers' Association Coventry 1938-1990: Political and Social Action, South Asian History and Culture, 2013, 4(4).

6. Goebel, S., Commemorative Cosmopolis: Transnational Networks of Remembrance in Post-war Coventry. in: Goebel, S. P. and Keene, D., eds., Cities into Battlefields: Metropolitan Scenarios, Experiences and Commemorations of Total War, Aldershot: Ashgate, 2011, pp. 163-183.

7. Gould, J. & C. Gould, Coventry: The Making of a Modern City 1939-1973, Historic England, 2016.

8. Healey, M. & D. Clark, Industrial Decline and Government Response in the West Midlands: The Case of Coventry, Regional Studies, 1984, 18(4), pp. 303-318.

9. Hodgkinson, G., Coventry and the Movement for World Peace: Writings and Speeches 1971-1975, Coventry: The Chapelfields Press, 1981.

10. Howard, R T., Ruined and Rebuilt: The Story of Coventry Cathedral 1939-1962, Letchworth: The Garden City Press Ltd, 1962.

11. Kaczka-Valliere, J. & A. Rigby, Coventry—Memorializing Peace and Reconciliation, Peace & Change, 2008, 33(4).

12. Kaczka-Valliere, J., A Study of Coventry's Mission for Peace and Reconciliation since the Second World War, PhD Thesis submitted to Coventry University, 2005.

13. Lamb, C., Reconciling People: Coventry Cathedral's Story, Norwich: Cantebury Press, 2011.

14. Lancaster, B. & Mason, T., eds., Life and Labour in a Twentieth Century City, Coventry: University of Warwick, Centre for the Study of Social History, 1986.

15. McGrory, D., Coventry's Blitz, Gloucestershire: Amberley Publishing, 2015.

16. McGrory, D., A Century of Coventry: Events, People and Places over the 20th Century, Stroud: The History Press, 2007.

17. Moulton, M., Ireland and the Irish in Interwar England, Cambridge: Cambridge University Press, 2014.

18. Newbold, E., Portrait of Coventry. Bury St. Edmunds: St. Edmundsbury Press, 1972.

19. Richardson, Kenneth., Twentieth-Century Coventry, Coventry: The Lanchester Polytechnic, 1972.

20. Rose, W. E., Sent from Coventry: A Mission of International Reconciliation, London: Oswald Wolff, 1980.

21. Smith, A., The City of Coventry: A Twentieth Century Icon, London: I. B. Tauris, 2006.

22. Spence, B. & H. Snoek, Out of the Ashes: A Progress through Coventry Cathedral, London: Geoffrey Bles Ltd, 1963.

23. Spence, B., Phoenix at Coventry, London: Geoffrey Bles Ltd, 1963.

24. Taylor, F., Coventry: Thursday, 14 November 1940, London: Bloomsbury, 2015.

25. Tiratsoo, N., Reconstruction, Affluence and Labour Politics: Coventry, 1945-1960 (Vol. 41), Abingdon: Routledge, 2019.

26. Walters, P., The Story of Coventry, Gloucestershire: The History Press, 2013.

27. Wright, K., Coventry—Cathedral of Peace: Healing the Wounds of History in International Reconciliation, Bloomington: Author House, 2012.

Acknowledgements

I would like to thank Professor Liu Cheng for the invitation to participate in this valuable book series, and for his patient encouragement throughout the project. Much gratitude is due to Luo Qingyun for her great assistance in carrying out historical research for this book, as well as Dr Bahar Baser for her helpful comments on the first draft and Pauline Harrowell for her careful proofreading of the final text.

For Photo Credits Please Refer to